·THE TASTE OF·
DESSERTS

SMITHMARK

Compiled by Frédéric Lebain and Jean-Paul Paireault
Photographed by Jean-Paul Paireault
Designed by Sue Cook
Adapted and Translated by Lynn Jennings-Collombet

Acknowledgements

The publishers would like to thank the following for their valuable assistance and cooperation in the production of this book:

Madam Bayle, at Mas Le Plan in Lourmarin, for facilities for location photography.
The shopkeepers of Lourmarin and Pertuis for their special efforts to obtain and provide a variety of fresh and attractive ingredients.
Monsieur Thomas, Faïencerie de Gien, Djan d'Harfeuille in Clamart, Morcrette, and Villeroy and Boch for the loan of glassware and plates.
Cine Photo Provence, in Aix-en-Provence for film processing.
Kettie Artigaud for her help with general styling and furnishing.
Kathleen Jennings for her patience and help throughout the adaptation and translation of this book.
Monsieur Remande, director of l'Ecole Supérieure de Cuisine in Paris.
Thanks are also due to Monsieur and Madame Lebain, Monsieur David and Madame Marie-Solange Bezaunt, Madame Chardot, and Monsieur Bernard Bouton of Sougé.

CLB 2359
This edition first published in the United States in 1991 by
SMITHMARK Publishers Inc.,
112 Madison Avenue, New York, NY 10016.
© 1991 Colour Library Books Ltd., Godalming, Surrey, England.
Typesetting by Inforum Typesetting, Portsmouth, England.
Color separations made in Singapore.
Printed by Tien Wah Press (PTE) Ltd, Singapore.
All rights reserved.
ISBN 0 8317 8651 5

SMITHMARK books are available for bulk purchase for sales promotion and premium use. For details write or telephone the Manager of Special Sales, SMITHMARK Publishers Inc., 112 Madison Avenue, New York, NY 10016. (212) 532-6600

·THE TASTE OF·
DESSERTS

Frederic Lebain · Jean Paul Paireault

Introduction

The word "dessert," says the dictionary, comes from the French verb *desservir* meaning "to clear the table," and describes "a usually sweet course served at the end of a meal." This definition may be strictly true but how inadequate it is for conveying the glorious self-indulgence of a true dessert. A wickedly rich chocolate charlotte or a creamy cheesecake may indeed end a meal, but they end it on a high note and do not merely serve as a springboard for clearing the table. That will be the last thing on the diner's mind!

The concept of desserts as we understand them, however, is a relatively modern one. Our ancestors had no means to indulge in sweet fantasies until that most basic of ingredients, refined sugar, became widely available in Europe and the New World in the eighteenth century. This marked the end of its long journey from India, where it had been known and used as early as 3000 BC. Even with the advent of sugar, the more usual ending to a European meal would be fruit, both fresh and dried, nuts and cheese, a tradition that was carried on in the New World.

The first, simple desserts encased the fruit and nuts in sweetened dough to produce pies and tarts, or combined eggs with sugar and milk or cream to produce custards and syllabubs. More substantial hot puddings included cereals or bread to satisfy the appetites of farmworkers and early pioneers. Increased refinement and delicacy in society demanded the same in cookery and eighteenth- and nineteenth-century Europe witnessed the zenith of desserts, as meals ended with a veritable cornucopia of sweet things: custards, pies, creams, cakes, pastries, meringues, gelatins, ice creams, and hot puddings. Americans took all these traditions, put them in the melting pot of the New World and added their own ideas, becoming the unrivaled dessert champions of the twentieth century.

We have now come almost full circle. Although there has never been such a wide variety of choices for the sweet-toothed cook, we are all realizing that such self-indulgence is too calorific and too rich for everyday eating. So, in the interests of a healthier diet, fresh fruit, nuts and cheese are returning as favorites for ending the ordinary, day-to-day meal.

However, any happy occasion – be it a birthday, an anniversary, the start of the weekend, passing an exam, dinner with friends, or any one of a million good reasons – requires celebrating. On such occasions only a real dessert will do; and on such occasions *The Taste of Desserts* is the cook's best friend, providing the means of cooking up a sweet dream that helps you to celebrate in style.

There are after all many people for whom the dessert is the whole point of a good meal. These are the people who always leave plenty of room when eating out so they can sample something from the dessert trolley. They are also the people who find it hard to forgive friends who provide just fresh fruit or cheese at the end of a dinner party – whatever the current thinking on healthy eating. If you are one of these people, or live with one, or simply count one among your friends (and who doesn't), *The Taste of Desserts* is the best means of pleasing them. Just choose any recipe from this delicious collection, follow it carefully and watch their faces light up. What if the dish is as likely to round out the eater as it rounds off the meal – it's back to the fruit and nuts tomorrow!

FRUIT-FILLED PINEAPPLE

*Coconut ice cream goes particularly well with this simple
fruit dessert.*

Step 1

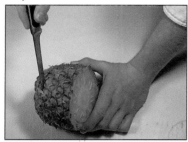

Step 1

Step 1

□ 1 large pineapple   □ 1 kiwi   □ 1 orange   □ ½ green apple
□ ½ red apple   □ 4 fresh figs   □ Few leaves fresh mint

1. Cut the top off the pineapple. Cut down all around the pineapple inside the skin. Cut a small slice from the bottom of the fruit and push out the pineapple flesh. Place the shell on a serving plate.

2. Dice the pineapple flesh neatly and evenly.

3. Peel the fruit, except for the apples, and slice or dice as appropriate. Mix the prepared fruit together.

4. Fill the shell with the prepared fruit and decorate with the fresh mint leaves. Serve any leftover fruit in a separate bowl for guests to help themselves.

□ TIME   Preparation takes about 30 minutes.

□ BUYING TIP   Using seasonal fruits will ensure that this recipe has many tasty variations.

□ WATCHPOINT   Do not forget to remove the brown "eyes" from the pineapple flesh.

□

OPPOSITE

FRUIT-FILLED
PINEAPPLE

—— SERVES 4 ——

CLAFOUTIS

*Clafoutis was baked at harvest time in central France to
satisfy appetites sharpened by a hard day's work in the fields.*

Step 1

Step 1

Step 3

Step 4

□ 5 tbsps all-purpose flour   □ 2 tbsps shredded coconut
□ 3 tbsps sugar   □ 5 eggs   □ 1 cup milk
□ 2 tsps butter, for greasing   □ 4 tbsps pie cherries

1. Beat the flour into the coconut together with the sugar and eggs. Add the milk a little at a time, beating well after each addition.

2. Butter one single or four individual pie pans.

3. Pour in the clafoutis batter, filling the pan(s) no more than three-quarters full.

4. Dot the cherries evenly over the mixture.

5. Bake in a moderate oven (350°F) for approximately 25 minutes.

6. Allow to cool completely before serving. The clafoutis will sink as it cools.

□ TIME   Preparation takes about 15 minutes and cooking takes approximately 25 minutes.

□ SERVING IDEA   If using canned cherries, serve with a little of the syrup from the can.

□ VARIATION   Different kinds of fruit can be used; adjust the quantity of sugar accordingly.

□

OPPOSITE

CLAFOUTIS

————— SERVES 4 —————

FRUIT-FILLED CRÊPES

Unusually, these delicious crêpes are served chilled.
The fruit filling could be varied according to taste and
what is in season.

Step 5

Step 6

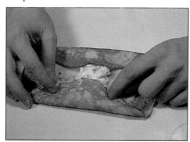

Step 6

Step 6

☐ 1¼ cups all-purpose flour ☐ 1 pinch salt ☐ 1½ eggs
☐ 2 tbsps sugar ☐ 1 cup milk ☐ 2 tbsps butter, softened
☐ 2 tbsps whipped cream ☐ 6 tbsps thick pastry cream
☐ 1 tsp orange liqueur ☐ 2 slices pineapple
☐ 1 small mango, peeled and pitted ☐ 1 kiwi
☐ 2 tangerines ☐ Oil

1. To make the crêpe batter, beat together the flour, salt, eggs and sugar. Add the milk gradually, beating well after each addition, to prevent lumps forming. When well mixed, beat in the softened butter. Set aside to rest for at least 15 minutes.

2. Fold the whipped cream into the pastry cream, then add the liqueur, stirring gently. Chill in the refrigerator.

3. Prepare all the fruit as necessary and chop into small cubes.

4. Cook the crêpes, regreasing the pan lightly with oil after each one. Leave the crêpes to cool.

5. Combine the prepared fruit with the pastry cream mixture.

6. Place a little filling down the center of each crêpe. Fold two sides of each crêpe up and over the filling. Roll up carefully so that the filling is kept in the center.

7. Chill the crêpes in the refrigerator before serving.

☐ TIME   Preparation takes about 30 minutes and cooking takes approximately 20 minutes, plus extra chilling time.

☐ SERVING IDEA   Serve with a chilled, crushed strawberry purée, dotted with whipped cream.

☐ WATCHPOINT   The above quantity of crêpe batter should make approximately 15 crêpes. Only 1-2 crêpes are required per person.

☐

OPPOSITE

FRUIT-FILLED
CRÊPES

—————— SERVES 4 ——————

FROMAGE FRAIS WITH STRAWBERRIES

*Many European countries boast desserts based on fruit and
soft cheeses and this tangy French recipe is one of the most
delicious – just right for rounding off a summer meal.*

Step 2

Step 3

□ 1½ cups strawberries, fresh or frozen   □ 1½ cups fromage frais
□ ¼ cup heavy cream   □ 3 tbsps sugar

---

1. Purée the strawberries either in a food processor or by passing
the fruit through a sieve.

2. Mix together the fromage frais, cream and sugar.

3. Stir in the strawberry purée and combine well.

4. Chill in the refrigerator, before serving.

□ TIME   Preparation takes about 10 minutes, plus extra chilling
time.

□ VARIATION   This recipe can be prepared using any type of
berry fruit.

□ BUYING TIP   The fromage frais can be replaced with sieved
cottage or Ricotta cheese.

□

OPPOSITE

FROMAGE FRAIS
WITH
STRAWBERRIES

SERVES 4

SPICED ORANGE SOUP

Fruit soups are popular in Europe; in some countries they are served as an appetizer, in other countries as a dessert – either way they make a refreshing dish.

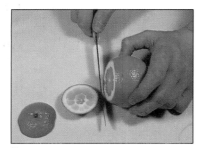

Step 1

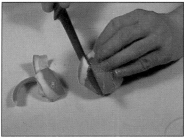

Step 1

Step 1

□ 4 oranges   □ 2 cups fresh orange juice   □ ¼ cup sugar
□ ¼ tsp cinnamon   □ 1 whole clove
□ ¼ vanilla bean

1. Using a sharp knife, peel the oranges, cutting down to the flesh. To section the orange, cut down between the flesh and the membrane, then remove each whole segment. Place the segments in a serving bowl.

2. Bring the orange juice to a boil with the sugar, cinnamon, clove and vanilla bean. Remove the whole spices by straining the hot, spicy juice over the orange segments.

3. Allow the soup to cool, then chill in the refrigerator for at least 2 hours before serving.

□ TIME   Preparation takes 15 minutes and cooking takes approximately 15 minutes, plus 2 hours chilling time.

□ SERVING IDEA   Serve the soup with balls of orange sherbert.

□ COOK'S TIP   The dish is much improved in appearance and taste if all the skin and pith are removed from the orange segments.

□

OPPOSITE

SPICED ORANGE
SOUP

———— SERVES 4 ————

CHERRY ZABAGLIONE

This extremely rich dessert, a variation on a classic Italian dish, could be served in smaller portions and accompanied by a fruit salad for the diet-conscious.

Step 1

Step 2

Step 3

□ 8 egg yolks   □ 3 tbsps sugar   □ 2 tbsps cherry juice
□ 20 pie cherries

1. Beat together the egg yolks with the sugar. Add the cherry juice and beat together thoroughly once more.

2. Place the bowl containing this mixture over a pan of boiling water and cook, beating continuously.

3. After a few minutes the mixture will thicken and increase in volume. Remove from heat and continue beating until cooled.

4. Serve in individual fruit dishes with the whole cherries.

□ TIME   Preparation takes 10 minutes and cooking takes approximately 15 minutes.

□ COOK'S TIP   To decorate, dip a fork in cherry juice and drizzle the juice over the zabaglione.

□ SERVING IDEA   Serve with almond or coconut cookies.

□

OPPOSITE

CHERRY
ZABAGLIONE

——— SERVES 4 ———

FRESH FRUIT IN
TULIP CUPS

*Elegant presentation in homemade tulip cups is what gives
this simple fruit dessert its special, dinner-party touch.*

Step 3

Step 3

Step 5

TULIP CUPS

☐ 1 egg white   ☐ ¼ cup sugar
☐ ¼ cup all-purpose flour   ☐ 2 tbsps butter, melted
☐ ¼ cup ground almonds   ☐ 1 tbsp flaked almonds

FRUIT FILLING

☐ 1 mango   ☐ 2 figs   ☐ 10 strawberries
☐ 1 kiwi   ☐ 10 cherries   ☐ 1 cup vanilla ice cream
☐ 1 tbsp flaked almonds

1. To make the tulip cups, mix the egg white with the sugar, then add the flour, melted butter and the ground almonds, beating well to incorporate all the ingredients. Set aside to rest for 1 hour.

2. Peel the fruit as necessary and cut into attractive shapes.

3. Place 1 tbsp of the batter on a non-stick cookie sheet, and spread it out well using the back of a spoon. Repeat three times. Sprinkle over 1 tbsp flaked almonds, dividing them equally between the four rounds.

4. Cook in a hot oven (400°F) for approximately 8-10 minutes, until lightly brown.

5. When cooked, and while they are still hot, mold the cookies by pressing them into brioche tins or small bowls. Allow them to cool and harden in the molds.

6. When cool, remove the tulip cups from their molds and place on serving plates. Fill with the fruit, top with a little vanilla ice cream and decorate with the remaining 1 tbsp flaked almonds.

☐ TIME   Preparation takes about 40 minutes, cooking takes 8-10 minutes and the cookie batter has to rest for 1 hour.

☐ SERVING IDEA   Serve with a fresh raspberry sauce: raspberries crushed with a little sugar and lemon juice.

☐ WATCHPOINT   The tulip shapes must be formed as soon as the cookies are removed from the hot oven, as they tend to harden very quickly.

☐ COOK'S TIP   As only four large tulips are needed for this recipe, use the remaining batter to make small almond cookies.

☐

OPPOSITE

FRESH FRUIT IN
TULIP CUPS

SERVES 6

FIGS IN SYRUP

*Fresh figs are a delicious and much underrated fruit, seen to
their best advantage in a simple recipe such as this one.*

Step 2

Step 3

□ 1¾ cups sugar   □ 4 cups water   □ 18 fresh figs
□ 3 tbsps fig liqueur, optional

1. In a small saucepan, bring the water and sugar to a boil.

2. Add the figs and the fig liqueur, if using, reduce the heat and simmer for about 35 minutes.

3. When the figs are tender, remove them using a slotted spoon and set aside in a bowl. Place the syrup back on the heat, and boil until reduced and thick.

4. Pour the thickened syrup over the figs and allow to cool. Chill before serving.

□ TIME   Preparation takes about 10 minutes and cooking takes approximately 35 minutes, plus extra chilling time.

□ SERVING IDEA   A fruit-flavored sorbet or ice cream complements this dish perfectly.

□ BUYING TIP   The purplish variety of figs are best for this recipe. Buy them while still firm, rather than too ripe.

□

OPPOSITE

FIGS IN SYRUP

DRIED FRUIT SALAD

*Soaking the fruit in sweet white wine gives a luxurious boost
to this winter standby.*

Step 1

Step 2

☐ Approximately 3 cups mixed dried fruit: pears, apricots,
sultanas, figs, dates, bananas or any other combination
☐ 1 bottle sweet white wine   ☐ 1-2 cups vanilla ice cream

1. Cut the larger fruit into small cubes.

2. Place all the fruit in a saucepan, pour over the wine and bring
to a boil.

3. As soon as the wine is boiling ignite the mixture with a match.
When the flames go out pour the fruit salad into a heatproof bowl
and allow to cool. When cool, place in the refrigerator to chill for
at least 2 hours.

4. Serve the fruit salad in shallow bowls with a small scoop of ice
cream.

☐ TIME   Preparation takes about 15 minutes, cooking takes
approximately 5 minutes and the fruit salad should be chilled for at
least 2 hours before serving.

☐ WATCHPOINT   Be very careful when igniting the wine as the
flames can go quite high.

☐ COOK'S TIP   Use Montbazillac white wine if available; if not,
a Sauternes or other sweet white wine is acceptable.

☐

OPPOSITE

DRIED FRUIT
SALAD

SERVES 4

GINGER-FLAVORED POACHED PEARS

The flavorsome combination of ginger and pears has long been recognized and this recipe shows the partnership off to its best advantage.

Step 2

Step 2

Step 3

☐ 4 ripe dessert pears   ☐ Juice of 1 lemon   ☐ 6 cups water
☐ ½ cup sugar   ☐ 1 tbsp ground ginger

1. Peel the pears and coat them liberally with the lemon juice.

2. Pour the water into a large saucepan, and add the sugar. Add the ginger and stir well.

3. Add the pears, cover the pan and poach the fruit over a moderate heat for approximately 30 minutes.

4. Once cooked, remove the pears from the pan and allow them to cool. Uncover the pan, increase the heat, and allow the cooking liquid to reduce until it thickens to a light syrup.

5. Allow the syrup to cool and serve it with the cooled pears.

☐ TIME   Preparation takes about 10 minutes and cooking takes approximately 1 hour 15 minutes.

☐ COOK'S TIP   Coating the pears with lemon juice prevents them from discoloring during cooking.

☐ VARIATION   Use more ginger for a stronger flavor or use cinnamon or whole cloves instead of ginger.

☐ WATCHPOINT   Poaching time will vary according to the ripeness of the pears. Check them from time to time and do not overcook.

☐

OPPOSITE

GINGER-
FLAVORED
POACHED PEARS

— SERVES 4 —

FRUIT SOUP WITH
MINT TEA

*Light and refreshing after a rich meal, this fruit soup could
also be served as an unusual summer appetizer.*

Step 1

Step 2

Step 3

☐ ¼ cup sugar   ☐ 2 cups water
☐ 4 mint-flavored herbal tea bags   ☐ ½ mango
☐ 2 figs   ☐ 10 cherries   ☐ 1 banana   ☐ 1 kiwi   ☐ 1 apple
☐ 2 oranges

1. Make a light caramel using the sugar and 2 tbsps of water (taken from the 2 cups).

2. When the caramel turns a light brown color, remove the pan from the heat and add the remaining water. Replace the pan on the heat and bring back to a boil.

3. Remove from the heat, add the tea bags and leave to infuse for 1 minute. Discard the tea bags.

4. Peel and trim the fruit as necessary, cutting into attractive shapes and placing in a bowl.

5. Add the caramel-flavored mint tea to the fruit and put in the refrigerator to chill for at least 12 hours.

6. Serve ice-cold.

☐ TIME   Preparation takes 25 minutes, cooking takes 10 minutes and the dish should be chilled for 12 hours before serving.

☐ WATCHPOINT   The caramel must not to be allowed to turn too brown, or it will give a bitter flavor to the tea.

☐ BUYING TIP   The mix of fruit can be varied according to what is available and more common varieties used in place of the exotic ones.

☐ COOK'S TIP   When adding the water to the hot caramel protect your hand and arm with a dishtowel.

☐

OPPOSITE

FRUIT SOUP
WITH MINT TEA

─── SERVES 4 ───

POACHED PEACHES WITH SPICES

Wine and spices add a touch of sophistication to a fruit dessert that is simplicity itself to make.

Step 1

Step 1

Step 2

Step 3

☐ 1 quart wine   ☐ 2 cups water   ☐ ½ cup sugar
☐ ½ vanilla bean   ☐ 1 juniper berry   ☐ 1 whole clove
☐ ½ tsp cinnamon   ☐ ¼ tsp powdered ginger
☐ 1 squeeze lemon juice   ☐ 4 peaches

1. Place the wine and water in a large saucepan or flameproof casserole. Stir in the sugar.

2. Add all the spices and a squeeze of lemon juice.

3. Add the peaches, cover the pan and poach the fruit on a gentle simmer, turning them from time to time.

4. After 30 minutes remove the peaches. Uncover the pan, increase the heat and allow the wine and spice mixture to reduce.

5. When the above has become thick and syrupy, strain through a fine sieve.

6. Cut the peaches into slices and arrange on four serving plates. Pour over the wine and spice sauce and chill in the refrigerator for at least 2 hours. Serve well chilled.

☐ TIME   Preparation takes about 10 minutes, cooking takes approximately 1 hour and the poached peaches should be chilled for at least 2 hours.

☐ BUYING TIP   It is best to use very firm peaches for this recipe. Cooking time will vary according to the type of peach.

☐

OPPOSITE

POACHED
PEACHES WITH
SPICES

——— SERVES 4 ———

FRUIT-FILLED MELON

A refreshing, easy-to-prepare dessert that relies on a colorful combination of different fruits for its effect.

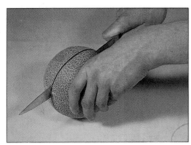

Step 1

Step 2

Step 3

☐ 2 melons ☐ 2 figs, cut into slices
☐ 1 green apple, thinly sliced ☐ 1 red apple, thinly sliced
☐ 1 kiwi, cut into round slices ☐ 1 orange, peeled
☐ 1 bunch grapes ☐ 12 raspberries ☐ Sugar

1. Cut the melons in half using a sharp knife. If desired, cut a thin slice off the bottom of the melon halves so that they are stable.

2. Scrape out the seeds with a small spoon and discard.

3. Using a melon-baller, cut five or six small balls from each melon half.

4. Cut the orange into segments and remove the skin. Wash and separate the grapes.

5. Put all the fruit, including the melon balls, into the melon halves.

6. Chill until ready to serve. A little sugar can be sprinkled over the fruit, if required.

☐ TIME   Preparation takes about 20 minutes.

☐ VARIATION   Use different fruit to fill the melons, according to season.

☐ COOK'S TIP   A spoonful of port makes a delicious addition to the fruit.

☐ BUYING TIP   Any type of melon can be used for this dish, so long as it is ripe.

☐

OPPOSITE

FRUIT-FILLED
MELON

—— SERVES 6 ——

CHOCOLATE CHEESECAKE

*The marbled effect of this chocolate-flavored cheesecake
means it looks as good as it tastes.*

Step 1

Step 6

Step 8

Step 9

☐ ½ cup sugar

☐ 1¼ cups fromage frais, or sieved cottage or Ricotta cheese

☐ 1 package gelatin   ☐ ½ cup heavy cream   ☐ 2 egg whites

☐ 4 tsps sugar   ☐ 4 oz unsweetened chocolate

☐ 3½ tbsps milk   ☐ Grated chocolate, to decorate

1. Beat the ½ cup sugar into the fromage frais until well mixed.

2. Soften the gelatin in a little cold water.

3. Whip the cream and leave to chill in the refrigerator.

4. Whip the egg whites with the remaining sugar until stiff.

5. Place the softened gelatin in a small bowl with 1-2 tsps water. Dissolve gently, either over a pan of boiling water or in a microwave oven. Mix into the fromage frais.

6. Fold the whipped cream into the fromage frais mixture.

7. Melt the chocolate with the milk, either over a pan of boiling water or in a microwave oven. Mix well.

8. Fold the egg whites gently but thoroughly into the fromage frais mixture.

9. Stir in the melted chocolate to create a marbled effect.

10. Pour into a ring or mold and leave to set for 2 hours in the refrigerator. Once the cheesecake has set, decorate with the grated chocolate and serve cold.

☐ TIME   Preparation takes about 35 minutes, plus approximately 2 hours setting time.

☐ COOK'S TIP   The gelatin can be dissolved in a saucepan over a low, direct heat, but add a further 2 tbsps water.

☐ WATCHPOINT   The egg whites must be folded very gently into the cheesecake mixture to increase its volume.

☐

OPPOSITE

CHOCOLATE
CHEESECAKE

—— SERVES 4 ——

CHOCOLATE FONDUE

A fondue is an essentially sociable form of eating that allows guests' appetites full rein and nothing could be more inviting than this fruit and chocolate version.

Step 2

Step 2

Step 2

□ 1 kiwi □ 2 slices pineapple □ 1 banana □ 1 green apple □ 1 red apple □ ⅔ cup litchis □ Small bunch grapes □ 2 oranges □ ½ mango □ 8 oz unsweetened chocolate □ ¾ cup heavy cream □ ½ cup milk □ 1 cup sugar

1. Prepare the fruit as necessary and cut into suitably sized chunks/slices.

2. Break the chocolate into a heavy-based saucepan and add the cream, milk and sugar. Place over a pan of boiling water and stir until the chocolate has melted and the mixture is smooth and shiny. If a more liquid sauce is preferred, stir in more cream. The chocolate may also be melted in a microwave.

3. Place the fruit around the pan containing the chocolate fondue and allow guests to help themselves, using a fork to dip pieces of fruit into the chocolate fondue mixture.

□ TIME   Preparation takes about 35 minutes and cooking takes approximately 5 minutes.

□ COOK'S TIP   The chocolate may require remelting, while the fondue is in progress. To do this, reheat it over boiling water or in the microwave, but not over direct heat as it will stick and burn.

□ BUYING TIP   The above list of fruit is just an indication; use any combination that is available.

□

OPPOSITE

CHOCOLATE
FONDUE

—— SERVES 6 ——

FROZEN DARK AND WHITE CHOCOLATE MOUSSE

Rich but irrestible, this dessert tastes every bit as good as it looks.

Step 4

Step 4

Step 4

- □ ½ cup bitter chocolate □ 3 tbsps heavy cream
- □ 4 tsps sugar □ 4 tsps butter □ 2 eggs, separated

- □ ¾ cup white chocolate □ 2 tbsps heavy cream
- □ 4 tsps sugar □ 4 tsps butter □ 2 eggs, separated

1. The method for making the two mousse mixtures is identical, but they must be made in separate bowls. Either over a pan of boiling water or in the microwave, melt the chocolate with the cream, sugar and butter.

2. Beat the egg yolks into each mixture.

3. Whip all four egg whites with a pinch of salt until stiff. Fold half into each mousse mixture.

4. Place six stainless steel rings or six ramekins on a freezerproof tray. Fill the rings/ramekins by layering in alternate tablespoonsful of the white and bitter chocolate mousse mixtures. Finish off the top layer by swirling the two colors together. Freeze for at least four hours.

5. Serve on plates decorated with a little grated chocolate, either removing the rings or leaving the mousses in the ramekins.

□ TIME Preparation takes about 35 minutes, cooking takes approximately 5 minutes and the mousse requires at least 4 hours to set/freeze.

□ COOK'S TIP For a softer mousse set in the refrigerator instead of the freezer.

□ WATCHPOINT The quantity of white chocolate used is slightly greater than that of the bitter chocolate as it hardens more slowly.

□

OPPOSITE

FROZEN DARK
AND WHITE
CHOCOLATE
MOUSSE

—— SERVES 8 ——

CHOCOLATE MARBLE CAKE

*This attractive cake is the ideal accompaniment to a fresh
fruit salad, but is also popular served on its own with coffee.*

Step 4

Step 4

Step 4

☐ 1½ cups softened butter   ☐ 1¾ cups sugar   ☐ 6 eggs
☐ 2 tsps baking powder   ☐ 3½ cups all-purpose flour
☐ 2 tbsps cocoa powder   ☐ ½ cup milk
☐ 1 tsp vanilla extract   ☐ 2 tbsps melted butter, for greasing

1. Cream the 1½ cups butter and the sugar together until very light. Beat in the eggs, baking powder and the flour, mixing well to obtain a smooth, thick cake batter.

2. Transfer one third of the batter to a clean bowl. Dissolve the cocoa powder in the milk, mix it into the batter and set aside.

3. Add the vanilla extract to the remaining cake batter.

4. Butter an oblong cake pan. Fill the bottom with half the white cake batter. Pour in the chocolate cake batter and then top with the remaining white batter. Swirl a knife through all the layers to create a marbled effect.

5. Bake in a moderate oven (335°F) for approximately 50 minutes, testing for doneness in the usual way. When cooked, turn the cake out onto a wire rack and allow to cool.

☐ TIME   Preparation takes about 25 minutes and cooking takes approximately 1 hour.

☐ COOK'S TIP   The white cake batter can be flavored with a few drops of orange flower water instead of the vanilla extract.

☐ VARIATION   Melted chocolate can used in place of the cocoa for a stronger flavor.

☐

OPPOSITE

CHOCOLATE
MARBLE CAKE

— SERVES 4 —

CHOCOLATE CHARLOTTE

Impress the chocolate-lovers in your life with this rich confection.

Step 1

Step 2

Step 3

□ 6 oz unsweetened chocolate □ ½ cup heavy cream
□ 3 tbsps sugar □ 3 tbsps butter □ 4 eggs, separated
□ 16 ladyfingers □ 2 tbsps rum □ 4 tbsps water

1. Combine the chocolate, cream, sugar and butter in a bowl. Place the bowl over a pan of boiling water to melt the ingredients.

2. Once melted, beat together well, adding the egg yolks one at a time and beating after each addition to incorporate thoroughly.

3. Beat the egg whites until very stiff, then fold carefully into the chocolate mixture.

4. Cut each ladyfinger in half. Mix together the rum and water. Dip each half ladyfinger quickly into the mixture.

5. Use the dipped ladyfingers to line four individual charlotte molds. Pour one quarter of the chocolate mixture into the center of each lined mold. Chill until set in the refrigerator, about 6 hours. Serve cold.

□ TIME   Preparation takes about 30 minutes, cooking takes approximately 10 minutes and the charlotte has to be chilled for at least 6 hours.

□ VARIATION   The mixture can be used to make one large charlotte, but a horizontal layer of biscuits should then be placed halfway down the chocolate filling.

□ WATCHPOINT   Cool the chocolate mixture for 5 minutes before folding in the stiffly beaten egg whites.

□

OPPOSITE

CHOCOLATE
CHARLOTTE

BANANA AND CHOCOLATE
TART

*This is a dessert that appeals particularly to children – aged
from eight to eighty!*

Step 5

Step 6

□ 2½ cups sweet pie dough □ 1 banana □ 2 tsps sugar
□ 1 squeeze lemon juice □ 8 oz semisweet chocolate
□ 4 tsps butter □ 4 tsps sugar □ 1 cup heavy cream

1. Roll out the dough and use to line a large pie pan. Bake 'blind' for 20 minutes in a hot oven (400°F). When cooked, remove the foil and the beans and allow to cool.

2. Mash the banana with the 2 tsps sugar and lemon juice and set aside.

3. Break the chocolate into smallish pieces, place in a large bowl with the butter and the 4 tsps sugar and set over a pan of boiling water, until the chocolate has melted.

4. Bring the cream to a boil and pour it over the chocolate. Whip the mixture well, then set aside.

5. Spread the banana mixture over the base of the cooked and cooled pie shell.

6. Pour the chocolate filling over the banana and spread evenly, using a spatula.

7. Chill in the refrigerator for at least 2 hours before serving.

□ TIME   Preparation takes about 1 hour, cooking takes approximately 30 minutes and the tart should be chilled for a minimum of 2 hours, preferably for 12 hours.

□ COOK'S TIP   For added flavor, mix a little banana liqueur into the banana, sugar and lemon juice.

□ SERVING IDEA   Serve with custard sauce flavored with rum and/or mixed with heavy cream.

□

OPPOSITE

BANANA AND
CHOCOLATE
TART

SERVES 6

CHOCOLATE RUM CAKE ROLL

This rich, gooey confection needs no accompaniment other than the compliments that always flow when it's brought to the table.

Step 1

Step 2

Step 3

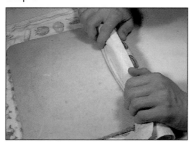

Step 3

□ 3 eggs □ 5 tbsps sugar □ 5 tbsps all-purpose flour
□ 2 tbsps melted butter □ 1 tbsp pastry cream
□ 6 tbsps rum □ 1 tbsp raisins □ 1 cup heavy cream
□ 1 heaping tbsp sugar □ 2 tbsps cocoa powder
□ Confectioners' sugar

1. In a bowl set over a pan of boiling water, beat the eggs with the 5 tbsps sugar until the mixture has thickened and forms threads when dropped from a spoon. Remove from the heat and continue to beat until the mixture has cooled.

2. Sprinkle over the flour a little at a time, folding it in gently. Fold in the melted butter.

3. Pour the batter into a greased and lined baking sheet, making sure it is evenly distributed, and bake in a hot oven (400°F) for 15 minutes, until firm but still springy to the touch. Turn out onto a slightly damp dishtowel and roll up tightly. Allow to cool for 1 hour.

4. Mix the pastry cream with the rum and raisins.

5. When the sponge has cooled completely unroll the dishtowel. The sponge tends to stick a little, so use a spatula if necessary to help separate it from the dishtowel.

6. Spread the pastry cream filling over the sponge, and roll it up again.

7. Whip the cream until thickened. Add the sugar and cocoa and whip again until stiff. Coat the roll all over with the cocoa cream. Use a fork to decorate the cream covering. Chill the roll in the refrigerator for 1 hour.

8. Sift a little confectioners' sugar and cocoa powder over the roll before serving.

□ TIME   Preparation takes about 30 minutes, plus 1 hour cooling time, and cooking takes approximately 15 minutes, plus 1 hour chilling time.

□ VARIATION   The cream may be flavored with a fruit liqueur instead of cocoa.

□

OPPOSITE

CHOCOLATE
RUM CAKE ROLL

—— SERVES 4 ——

CHOCOLATE SOUFFLÉ

*A featherlight soufflé is always a popular dessert – flavor it
with chocolate and it's a definite winner!*

Step 2

Step 3

Step 4

☐ Melted butter   ☐ Sugar   ☐ 1½ eggs   ☐ Scant ½ cup sugar
☐ 2 tbsps flour   ☐ 1 heaping tbsp cocoa powder
☐ 1 cup milk   ☐ 1 egg yolk   ☐ 4 egg whites   ☐ Salt
☐ Confectioners' sugar

1. Grease four ramekins with the melted butter, and sprinkle with sugar, shaking out any excess.

2. Beat the eggs with the sugar and then beat in the flour and the cocoa powder.

3. Bring the milk to a boil, then pour it over the egg mixture, stirring continuously.

4. Return the mixture to the saucepan and stir continuously over low heat until it has thickened and is just coming to a boil. Remove from the heat and allow to cool. When cool, add the egg yolk and mix in well.

5. Beat the egg whites with a pinch of salt until stiff. Mix a little of the egg white into the soufflé mixture to lighten it and then fold in the remaining egg white gently but thoroughly.

6. Fill the ramekins with the soufflé mixture and bake in a hot oven (400°F) for about 20 minutes, until well risen and firm. Remove from the oven, sprinkle quickly with confectioners' sugar and serve immediately, before the soufflés fall.

☐ TIME   Preparation takes about 30 minutes and cooking takes approximately 20 minutes.

☐ WATCHPOINT   Fold the egg whites very gently into the soufflé mixture, so that they retain their volume.

☐ COOK'S TIP   The cream mixture can be prepared a few hours in advance and the egg whites added at the last moment.

☐

OPPOSITE

CHOCOLATE
SOUFFLÉ

BLACK FOREST GATEAU

Originally a southern German coffee cake, this gateau is a chocolate-lover's delight that makes a winning dessert in this less traditional version.

Step 7

Step 8

Step 9

Step 10

□

OPPOSITE

BLACK FOREST
GATEAU

CAKE BATTER
□ 2 cups all-purpose flour   □ 4 tbsps chocolate powder
□ 4 eggs   □ 5½ tbsps sugar   □ 1 tbsp baking powder
□ 2 tbsps oil   □ ¾ cup milk

DARK CHOCOLATE FILLING
□ 2 cups chocolate powder   □ Scant ½ cup heavy cream
□ 3 tbsps sugar   □ 3 tbsps butter   □ 4 eggs, separated

WHITE CHOCOLATE FILLING
□ ½ cup white chocolate   □ ½ cup heavy cream
□ 1 tbsp raisins or currants   □ 2 tbsps rum

1. To make the basic cake, mix the flour with the chocolate powder, eggs, sugar, baking powder and 1 tbsp of the oil. Gradually add the milk, mixing in well.

2. Grease a round, high-sided cake pan (the cake rises during cooking) with the remaining oil and pour in the cake batter. Cook in a steamer for 35 minutes. When cooked, allow to cool slightly before turning out onto a wire rack to cool completely.

3. To make the dark chocolate filling, mix together the chocolate powder, cream, sugar and butter in a saucepan over simmering water. When melted, mix well and beat in the 4 egg yolks. Whip the egg whites until stiff.

4. For the white chocolate filling, finely chop the chocolate. Bring the cream to the boil and then pour it over the chocolate, stirring well until the chocolate has melted. Stir in the raisins.

5. Mix the rum with 2 tbsps of water.

6. Cut the cake into four equal layers and brush a little of the rum and water mixture over each one.

7. Place a metal cake ring on a serving plate and place one round of cake in the bottom.

8. Fold the egg whites into the dark chocolate filling. Spread half over the bottom layer of cake.

9. Place a second layer of cake over the dark chocolate filling. Top with the white chocolate filling and then add another cake layer.

10. Pour in the remaining dark chocolate filling and cover with the final cake layer. Chill for at least 2 hours in the refrigerator.

11. Remove the metal cake ring, decorate the cake with grated chocolate and ground coconut and serve.

□ TIME   Preparation takes about 40 minutes, steaming takes 35 minutes and the cake should be chilled for at least 2 hours before serving.

—— SERVES 4 ——

BANANA FRITTERS

*These delicious fritters make the perfect end to a spicy meal,
and are also much loved by children at any time.*

Step 1

Step 1

Step 1

☐ 1¼ cups all-purpose flour   ☐ 1 tsp yeast   ☐ ½ cup warm milk
☐ 2 pinches salt   ☐ 1 egg   ☐ 2 tbsps oil   ☐ 2 bananas
☐ Oil for deep-frying   ☐ Confectioners' sugar   ☐ Cinnamon

1. Place the flour in a bowl and mix in the yeast and the warm milk. Stir in the salt, egg and the 2 tbsps oil. Mix well to obtain a thick but light batter. Leave to rest in a warm place for 1 hour.

2. Peel the bananas, slice each in half lengthwise and then twice crosswise, to obtain six pieces from each banana.

3. Heat the oil for deep-frying. Dip each banana piece in the batter and then drop into the hot oil.

4. Turn the fritters over during cooking. When the fritters are crisp and golden, drain them on paper towels, sift over a mixture of confectioners' sugar and cinnamon and serve immediately.

☐ TIME   Preparation takes about 20 minutes, plus 1 hour resting time, and cooking takes approximately 5 minutes.

☐ COOK'S TIP   Dip the banana pieces in sugar first to give the fritters extra sweetness.

☐ WATCHPOINT   The oil should be hot enough to cook the fritters through without burning the outside.

☐

OPPOSITE

BANANA
FRITTERS

— SERVES 4 —

SAUTÉED APPLES WITH CALVADOS

This dessert uses two of the Normandy region's most famous products to create a true taste of France.

Step 2

Step 3

Step 4

☐ 4 small apples   ☐ 2 tbsps butter   ☐ 2 tbsps sugar
☐ ¼ cup flaked almonds   ☐ 2 tbsps raisins
☐ 2 tbsps Calvados

1. Peel the apples and cut them into even-sized pieces.

2. Heat the butter and add the apples. Sauté until lightly colored then add the sugar.

3. Add the almonds and raisins and sauté for a further 2 minutes.

4. Flame the mixture with the Calvados, sauté for a further minute and serve immediately.

☐ TIME   Preparation takes about 15 minutes and cooking approximately 10 minutes.

☐ SERVING IDEA   A custard sauce flavored with cinnamon would go particularly well with this dish.

☐ VARIATION   Try different liqueurs: rum, Armagnac etc.

☐ WATCHPOINT   Take care when you flame the sautéed apples as the flame can go quite high.

☐

OPPOSITE

SAUTÉED
APPLES WITH
CALVADOS

—— SERVES 4 ——

FRESH FRUIT GRATIN

*A creamy, caramelized topping covers a delicious
combination of exotic fruit in this fresh fruit gratin.*

Step 1

Step 1

Step 1

□ 1 egg yolk   □ 4 tbsps pastry cream
□ ½ tbsp kirsch or other fruit liqueur (optional)
□ 2 tbsps whipped cream, unsweetened   □ 1 mango
□ 4 figs   □ 1 kiwi

1. Mix the egg yolk into the pastry cream, then add the kirsch, if using, mixing it in well. Using a spatula, gently fold in the whipped cream.

2. Peel the fruit as necessary and cut into suitable chunks. Divide the fruit equally between four ovenproof dishes. Arranging the fruit attractively is not important as it is covered by the cream.

3. Cover the fruit with the creamy topping and place under a hot broiler. Brown lightly and serve immediately.

□ TIME   Preparation takes about 15 minutes and cooking takes approximately 5 minutes.

□ WATCHPOINT   The gratin colors very quickly under a hot broiler, so watch it carefully.

□

OPPOSITE

FRESH FRUIT

GRATIN

SERVES 4

INDIVIDUAL BLUEBERRY CRUMBLES

Crumbles make good, filling fall puddings; baking them in individual portions and serving them with vanilla ice cream or heavy cream takes them out of the everyday.

Step 1

Step 1

Step 2

Step 2

□ 4 tbsps all-purpose flour   □ ½ tsp baking powder
□ ¼ cup sugar   □ ¼ cup butter
□ 4 tbsps frozen blueberries, with their juice   □ 4 tbsps sugar
□ 2 apples   □ Cinnamon

1. Add the baking powder to the flour. Stir in the ¼ cup sugar and mix thoroughly with the flour and baking powder.

2. Rub in the butter using your fingertips until the mixture is crumbly. Set aside in the refrigerator until needed.

3. Divide the blueberries between four ramekins, or place in one large dish if preferred. Sprinkle the 4 tbsps sugar evenly over the blueberries.

4. Peel and core the apples then cut them into small cubes. Place these over the bluberries and sprinkle with cinnamon.

5. Top with the crumble mixture and cook in a moderate oven (350°F) for 20 minutes. Serve warm.

□ TIME   Preparation takes about 20 minutes and cooking also takes about 20 minutes.

□ VARIATION   When in season, use blackberries in place of the blueberries.

□

OPPOSITE

INDIVIDUAL
BLUEBERRY
CRUMBLES

——— SERVES 4 ———

BRIOCHE FRENCH TOASTS

These brioche French toasts make an unusual dessert, but
could also be served for an extra-special breakfast dish, with
or without the vanilla custard sauce.

Step 2

Step 3

Step 4

☐ 4 small brioches   ☐ 4 tbsps heavy cream   ☐ 3 eggs
☐ 1 tbsp sugar   ☐ 1 tsp orange flower water   ☐ 2 tbsps butter
☐ Confectioners' sugar   ☐ Vanilla custard sauce

1. Cut each small brioche into three slices.

2. Beat together the cream, eggs, sugar, and orange flower water.

3. Dip each brioche slice quickly into the cream and egg mixture, making sure both sides are coated.

4. Heat a little of the butter at a time and sauté the dipped slices in batches, cooking the toasts for about two minutes on each side, until golden brown.

5. Serve each batch immediately, sprinkled with a little sifted confectioners' sugar and surrounded by the vanilla custard sauce.

☐ TIME   Preparation takes about 5 minutes and cooking takes approximately 4 minutes for each batch.

☐ VARIATION   White bread can be used if brioches are not available.

☐ COOK'S TIP   Serve the brioche French toasts as soon as they have been cooked as they tend to dry out quickly.

☐

OPPOSITE

BRIOCHE
FRENCH TOASTS

—————— SERVES 4 ——————

APPLE FRITTERS

When apples abound in fall and ideas for cooking them
are running out, try these delicious fritters – they're sure to be
a success.

Step 4

Step 5

Step 6

□ 1¼ cups all-purpose flour □ 1 tsp yeast □ ½ cup warm milk
□ 1 egg □ 5 tsps oil □ 2 pinches salt □ 4 small apples
□ Oil for deep-frying □ Confectioners' sugar

1. Sift the flour into a mound, make a hollow in the center and place the yeast in it. Pour in the warm milk.

2. Add the egg, the 5 tsps oil and the salt and mix all the ingredients together well. Leave to rest in a warm place for 1 hour.

3. Peel and core the apples. Cut into pieces.

4. Heat the oil for deep-frying. Using a fork, dip the apple pieces into the batter.

5. Drop the fritters into the hot oil.

6. When golden brown, strain out of the oil and drain on paper towels. Serve warm, sprinkled with confectioners' sugar.

□ TIME   Preparation takes 20 minutes, plus 1 hour resting time, and cooking takes a few minutes per batch of fritters.

□ COOK'S TIP   Use slightly acidic cooking apples, and dip the pieces in sugar and cinnamon before dipping them in the batter.

□ WATCHPOINT   If the apple fritters do not turn over naturally during frying, turn them with a fork, so that they cook evenly.

□

OPPOSITE

APPLE FRITTERS

SAUTÉED CRÊPES À L'ORANGE

Similar in method to the famous Crêpes Suzette, this impressive dessert requires last-minute cooking but brings the compliments flooding in.

Step 4

Step 5

Step 6

Step 6

CRÊPE BATTER
- ☐ 1¼ cups all-purpose flour ☐ Pinch salt ☐ 1½ eggs
- ☐ 2 tbsps sugar ☐ 1 cup milk ☐ ⅛ cup butter, softened

FILLING
- ☐ 6 tbsps sugar ☐ 2 tbsps butter ☐ ¼ cup Grand Marnier
- ☐ 1 cup orange juice

1. To make the crêpe batter, mix together the flour, salt, eggs and sugar. Gradually add the milk, beating well. Add the softened butter, beat in well, then set the batter aside to rest for 15 minutes.

2. Cook the crêpes in a little hot oil, lightly regreasing the pan after each one has been cooked, until all the batter has been used up.

3. Boil the butter and sugar together to make a light-colored caramel.

4. Add the Grand Marnier off the heat, taking care to avoid splattering.

5. Stir in the orange juice. Return the pan to the heat and bring to a boil. Cook until the sauce has reduced to a light syrup.

6. Allow two crêpes per person. Dip each crêpe in the sauce, fold it in quarter and serve warm.

☐ TIME   Preparation takes about 40 minutes and cooking takes approximately 35 minutes.

☐ WATCHPOINT   The sauce should be well reduced and syrupy before dipping in the crêpes.

☐ COOK'S TIP   Just before dipping the crêpes in the sauce, reheat them quickly in a hot oven or a microwave.

☐ VARIATION   Grapefruit juice with gin is a tasty alternative to the orange juice/Grand Marnier combination.

☐

OPPOSITE

SAUTÉED
CRÊPES À
L'ORANGE

——— SERVES 4 ———

FRENCH TOAST WITH RAISINS

Serving these fruity French toasts with a rum-flavored custard sauce adds a touch of sophistication to an otherwise simple dessert.

□ 2 tbsps raisins   □ 1 tbsp rum   □ 2 eggs
□ ½ cup heavy cream   □ 8 slices white bread
□ 2 tbsps butter   □ Sugar

Step 3

Step 4

Step 5

1. Marinate the raisins in the rum.

2. Beat the eggs with the cream.

3. Soak each slice of bread in the egg mixture for a few seconds on both sides.

4. Heat a little of the butter in a frying pan, add the egged bread in batches and cook for a few minutes on one side.

5. Top each slice with a few of the marinated raisins then turn to cook the other side.

6. When cooked on both sides, place on a serving plate, sprinkle with sugar and serve immediately.

□ TIME   Preparation takes about 10 minutes and cooking takes approximately 7 minutes.

□ COOK'S TIP   Use thick slices of soft bread for the best results.

□ VARIATION   Use candied fruit instead of raisins.

□

OPPOSITE

FRENCH TOAST
WITH RAISINS

——— SERVES 4 ———

CRÈME BRÛLÉE WITH ALMONDS

*Flavoring this classic dessert with almonds adds to its
delicious richness.*

Step 1

Step 2

Step 3

□ 3 eggs   □ 2 cups heavy cream   □ 2 tbsps sugar
□ 5 drops almond extract, or more to taste
□ 4 tsps ground almonds   □ 3-4 tbsps sugar

---

1. Beat the eggs with the cream and the 2 tbsps sugar.

2. Add the almond extract and mix it in well.

3. Add the ground almonds, stir in well and pour into a shallow ovenproof dish.

4. Place the dish in a baking pan filled with water and cook in a low oven (300°F) for approximately 40 minutes.

5. Allow to cool and then put in the refrigerator to chill. Just before serving sprinkle the remaining sugar over the chilled custard in a thin, even layer. Caramelize under a hot broiler, watching the dish carefully and turning it if need be so the sugar browns evenly.

□ TIME   Preparation takes about 15 minutes, plus extra chilling time, and cooking takes approximately 40 minutes.

□ DIET TIP   To obtain a less rich custard, use half milk, half cream.

□ VARIATION   Different flavored custards can be obtained by replacing the almond extract either with a liqueur or with vanilla extract.

□

OPPOSITE

CRÈME BRÛLÉE
WITH ALMONDS

——— SERVES 4 ———

HONEY CUSTARDS

Honey adds a very distinctive touch to these little baked custards – try using one of the more exotic varieties for extra flavor.

Step 3

Step 4

Step 5

Step 6

□ ¼ vanilla bean   □ 2 scant cups milk   □ 5 egg yolks
□ Scant ½ cup honey

1. Cut open the vanilla bean lengthwise. Run a knife down the inside of the bean to remove the seeds.

2. Bring the milk to a boil with the vanilla bean and seeds.

3. Beat together the egg yolks and honey.

4. Pour the boiling milk onto the beaten egg mixture, stirring continuously until well mixed.

5. Allow the custard to stand for 15 minutes, then skim the surface.

6. Strain the custard into four ramekins and place them in a baking pan of water.

7. Cook the custards in a low oven (300°F) for about 40 minutes, or until the blade of a knife, inserted into the edge of the custard, comes out clean. Remove the custards from the oven and allow to cool.

8. Once cool, chill the custards in the refrigerator until ready to serve. Do not turn them out but eat the custards directly from the ramekins.

□ TIME   Preparation takes about 10 minutes, plus 15 minutes standing time, and cooking takes approximately 40 minutes, plus extra chilling time.

□ SERVING IDEA   Top the custards with a small spoonful of jam just before serving.

□ VARIATION   The honey can be replaced with sugar to make a more conventional custard.

□ WATCHPOINT   Cooking must be done in a low oven for optimum results.

□

OPPOSITE

HONEY
CUSTARDS

---- SERVES 6 ----

FRENCH BREAD PUDDING
WITH FRUIT

*An old nursery favorite is given a sophisticated new look that
would make it welcome at any dinner table.*

Step 3

Step 3

Step 4

Step 5

□ 3 tbsps candied fruit □ 3 tbsps raisins □ 3 tbsps kirsch
□ 3 cups milk □ ½ cup sugar
□ ½ vanilla bean, cut open lengthwise
□ 3 cups bread, crusts removed
□ 5 eggs □ 2 tsps butter

1. Marinate the candied fruit and raisins in the kirsch.

2. Bring the milk and sugar to a boil with the vanilla bean.

3. Crumble the bread into a bowl. Remove the vanilla bean from
the hot milk and pour the hot milk and sugar over the bread. Place
in a food processor and mix until smooth.

4. Stir in the eggs, marinated fruit and the kirsch and mix together
well.

5. Butter a charlotte mold and fill with the bread pudding mixture.
Bake in a hot oven (420°F) for approximately 50 minutes. When
the blade of a knife slipped into the pudding comes out clean, the
pudding is done.

6. Allow to cool before turning out onto a serving plate. Decorate
with a little whipped cream before serving.

□ TIME   Preparation takes 30 minutes and cooking takes
approximately 50 minutes.

□ SERVING IDEA   Serve with custard sauce.

□ VARIATION   Use different dried fruits, or nuts, and liqueurs;
for instance, dried apricots and apricot brandy.

□

OPPOSITE

FRENCH BREAD
PUDDING WITH
FRUIT

——— SERVES 4 ———

COCONUT FLAN

Coconut adds extra sweetness to a simple dessert that will appeal to all the family.

Step 1

Step 2

Step 3

□ ¼ cup all-purpose flour   □ 2 eggs   □ 2 egg yolks
□ 1 tbsp coconut liqueur   □ 2 cups milk
□ ½ cup shredded coconut   □ Few drops vanilla extract
□ ¼ cup sugar   □ 2 tsps melted butter
□ Melted chocolate, thinned with a little milk

1. Mix together the flour, eggs, egg yolks and coconut liqueur.

2. Put the milk on to boil with the shredded coconut, vanilla extract and the sugar, stirring the mixture carefully. When it comes to a boil, remove from the heat and beat it into the egg mixture.

3. Use the melted butter to grease a cake pan or shallow baking dish. Pour in the flan mixture.

4. Cook in a shallow pan filled with hot water in a moderately hot oven (350°F) for about 40 minutes.

5. Remove from the oven. Allow to cool completely before turning out and serving decorated with the thinned melted chocolate.

□ TIME   Preparation takes about 15 minutes and cooking takes approximately 40 minutes, plus extra cooling time.

□ COOK'S TIP   To test for doneness, insert the blade of a knife into the center of the flan; if it comes out clean the flan is cooked.

□ WATCHPOINT   Stir the milk mixture as it comes to a boil to prevent the coconut from sticking.

□

OPPOSITE

COCONUT FLAN

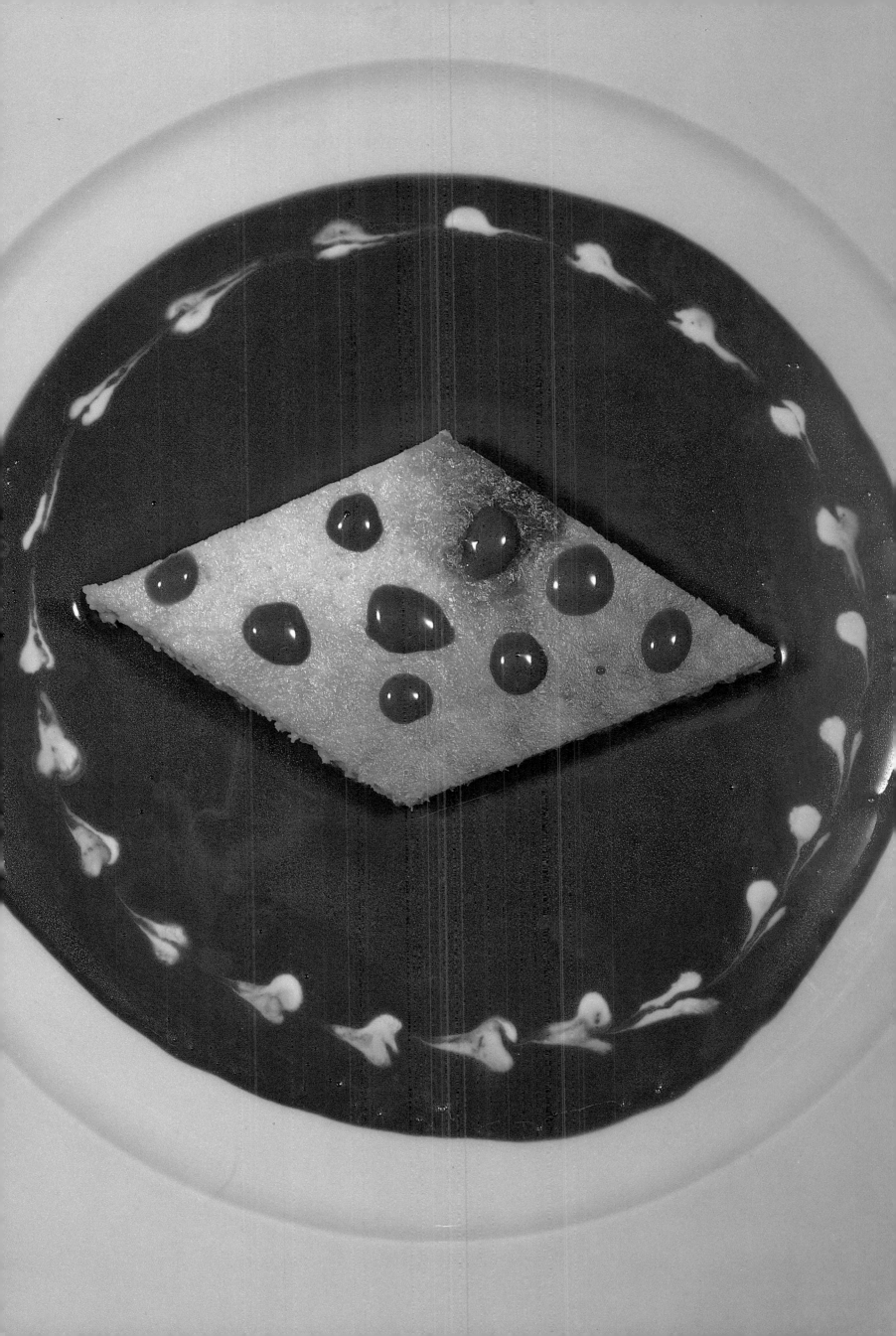

—————— SERVES 4 ——————

RICE PUDDING

This pudding is extremely popular in Europe, where it has been served to generations of children. Discover a grown-up taste for it with this recipe.

Step 6

Step 7

□ ¾ cup long-grain rice   □ 3¼ cups milk
□ ½ cup sugar   □ ¼ vanilla bean   □ 3 egg yolks
□ Cinnamon to taste

1. Rinse the rice in water and set aside to drain.

2. Place the rice in a pan, cover it with water, and boil on a high heat for 1 minute. Drain.

3. Bring the milk to a boil with the sugar and vanilla. Stir in the rice. Transfer the rice mixture into an ovenproof dish, cover with aluminum foil and finish cooking in a moderate oven (325°F) for 20-30 minutes, until the rice is soft but the milk has not completely evaporated.

4. Remove the vanilla bean and rapidly beat the egg yolks into the rice mixture.

5. Pour the mixture onto a large plate, so that the pudding mixture will cool rapidly.

6. When cool, divide the rice pudding between four ramekins or small bowls, flattening the mixture with the back of a spoon.

7. Sprinkle cinnamon to taste over the puddings and serve cold. The puddings may also be served warm, by omiting Step 5.

□ TIME   Preparation takes about 35 minutes and cooking takes approximately 30 minutes.

□ VARIATION   Marinate some dried fruit in an appropriate liqueur, e.g. raisins in rum, and add at Step 4.

□ BUYING TIP   Use long-grain rather than the more usual short-grain rice for this recipe.

□

OPPOSITE

RICE PUDDING

―――― SERVES 4 ――――

CHESTNUT CREAMS

*Simple to make yet luscious to eat, this rich, smooth dessert is
not set with gelatin, giving it a particularly creamy texture.*

Step 1

☐ 1¼ cups sweetened chestnut purée with vanilla
☐ 1¼ cups fromage frais   ☐ ¾ cup whipping cream
☐ 1 tbsp Marasquin   ☐ 2-3 candied chestnuts, chopped

1. Mix together the chestnut purée and the fromage frais.

2. Whip the cream until thickened and stir in the Marasquin.
Gently fold the cream into the chestnut and fromage frais mixture.

3. Spoon the chestnut cream carefully into individual serving
dishes or coupes and decorate with the chopped candied
chestnuts. Chill for 1 hour before serving.

☐ TIME   Preparation takes about 10 minutes, plus chilling time of
1 hour.

☐ COOK'S TIP   Vanilla-flavored chestnut purée, which is
available from specialty food shops, is already sweet; however, sugar
may be added to the whipping cream if an even sweeter taste is
preferred.

☐ BUYING TIP   Sweetened chestnut purée is an import from
France available in specialty food shops.

☐ VARIATION   If fromage frais is not available, use sieved
cottage or Ricotta cheese. The Marasquin, or chestnut liqueur, may be
replaced with brandy and chestnuts in syrup could be used in place of
the candied chestnuts.

☐

OPPOSITE

CHESTNUT
CREAMS

SERVES 4

MALAKOFF AUNT IDA

*This simple nursery-style pudding is easy to digest after
a rich meal.*

Step 3

Step 5

Step 7

□ 4 egg yolks □ 3½ tbsps sugar □ ½ tsp vanilla extract
□ ¼ cup cornstarch □ 1 cup milk □ 4 egg whites
□ ½ cup sugar □ 3 tbsps water

1. Mix together the egg yolks, the 3½ tbsps sugar, the vanilla extract and cornstarch.

2. Bring the milk to a boil and stir it into the above mixture. Pour the pastry cream back into the saucepan, replace on a gentle heat and stir continuously until thick.

3. Pour the pastry cream into a heatproof glass serving dish and allow to cool.

4. Make a caramel with the ½ cup sugar and the water. When lightly colored carefully pour in a scant ½ cup of water. Reheat to dissolve the caramel, which will now remain liquid.

5. Pour half the caramel over the pastry cream and spread evenly.

6. Beat the egg whites until foamy. Pour in the remaining caramel, beating continuously to obtain a stiff meringue mixture.

7. Pipe the meringue onto the caramel-topped pastry cream. Sift over a little chocolate powder and serve immediately, otherwise the egg whites will fall.

□ TIME   Preparation and cooking take a total of about 40 minutes.

□

OPPOSITE

MALAKOFF
AUNT IDA

─────── SERVES 4 ───────

CINNAMON TAGLIATELLE

*A homemade, sweetened pasta forms the basis of this
decidedly different dessert.*

Step 3

Step 4

Step 4

Step 4

☐ 2 cups all-purpose flour   ☐ 2 tbsps sugar   ☐ 1 tsp cinnamon
☐ 2 eggs   ☐ 2 cups milk   ☐ 2 cups custard sauce

1. To make the pasta, mix together the flour, sugar, cinnamon and eggs. The amount of cinnamon may be varied to taste. Work the dough into a ball and set aside to rest for 30 minutes.

2. Prepare the pasta machine rollers, or flour the work surface if using a rolling pin.

3. Feed the dough through the rollers, or roll out very thinly, flouring the utensils liberally throughout.

4. Roll the strips through the cutter to form tagliatelle, or cut into thin bands with a sharp knife. Allow to dry for at least 2 hours.

5. Bring the milk to a boil with plenty of water, and cook the tagliatelle *al dente* as for traditional pasta, stirring once or twice to prevent sticking.

6. Drain and rinse the cooked pasta. Allow to cool.

7. When cool, mix into the custard sauce and serve, sprinkled with a little extra cinnamon.

☐ TIME   Preparation takes 45 minutes, plus 2 hours resting time, and cooking takes 6-8 minutes.

☐ WATCHPOINT   Flour all the utensils well during the rolling and cutting, as the sugar makes the dough sticky and fragile.

☐ SERVING IDEA   The tagliatelle could also be served with a fresh fruit purée.

☐

OPPOSITE

CINNAMON
TAGLIATELLE

—— SERVES 4 ——

SEMOLINA CAKE WITH DRIED FRUIT

An English nursery pudding is updated with the addition of orange flower water and dried fruit.

Step 1

Step 2

Step 3

☐ 2 cups milk ☐ 1 tbsp orange flower water ☐ 2 tbsps sugar
☐ 4 tbsps finely ground semolina
☐ Approximately ½ cup dried fruit, diced as necessary
☐ 1 egg yolk

1. In a saucepan, mix the milk with the orange flower water and the sugar. Bring to a boil.

2. Pour the semolina into the boiling milk, stirring rapidly.

3. Add the dried fruit and cook the mixture for approximately 6-8 minutes, stirring continuously.

4. When cooked, remove from the heat and beat in the egg yolk.

5. Pour into a single serving bowl or divide between four small ramekins and chill for at least 1 hour in the refrigerator before serving.

☐ TIME   Preparation takes 15 minutes, cooking takes 10 minutes and the dish should be chilled for at least 1 hour.

☐ SERVING IDEA   Turn the semolina cakes out onto serving plates and surround with a custard sauce, flavored with orange flower water, and chopped dried fruit.

☐ COOK'S TIP   A heavier cake can be made by using a little more semolina.

☐ WATCHPOINT   While the semolina is cooking, it must be stirred continuously to prevent it sticking and burning.

☐

OPPOSITE

SEMOLINA CAKE
WITH DRIED
FRUIT

—— SERVES 4 ——

FLOATING ISLANDS

*Many countries claim this dessert as their own – which
simply proves how deservedly popular it is.*

Step 1

Step 1

Step 3

Step 4

☐ 6 egg whites   ☐ Pinch of salt   ☐ ½ cup sugar
☐ 2 cups milk   ☐ 2 cups water   ☐ 2 cups custard sauce
☐ 2 tbsps crushed praliné

---

1. Whip the egg whites with a pinch of salt until light and foamy. Add half the sugar and whip until nearly stiff. Add the remaining sugar and continue whipping until stiff peaks form.

2. Heat the milk and water together over a moderate heat.

3. Place the meringue mixture in a pastry bag without a nozzle and squeeze large "islands" of meringue out onto a spatula. If you do not have a pastry bag, simply use a tablespoon to scoop out the islands and drop them directly into the hot milk and water.

4. Lower each meringue island into the hot milk and water on the spatula and gently poach the meringue islands for about 2 minutes, turning once. Poaching time will depend on the islands' size. However, do not poach for too long or they will dissolve.

5. Lift the islands out of the milk and water using a slotted spoon and leave to drain and cool on a wire rack.

6. To serve, divide the custard sauce between four serving dishes, place the meringue islands on top, sprinkle over the crushed praliné and serve.

☐ TIME   Preparation takes about 20 minutes and cooking takes approximately 5 minutes, plus extra cooling time.

☐ SERVING IDEA   The floating islands can also be decorated by using a fork to drizzle over a little caramel.

☐ WATCHPOINT   The sugared egg whites must be very firm and creamy before poaching in the milk and water.

☐ BUYING TIP   Praliné is a type of nut brittle which can be purchased in specialty food shops or made at home.

☐

OPPOSITE

FLOATING
ISLANDS

—— SERVES 4 ——

ORANGE FLOWER CRÈME CARAMEL

*Orange flower water gives a delicate flavor to these custards,
although they may also be flavored with the more traditional
vanilla extract, if preferred.*

Step 3

Step 4

Step 5

□ 3 eggs   □ 1 egg yolk   □ Scant ½ cup sugar
□ 2 tbsps orange flower water   □ 2 cups milk
□ ½ cup sugar   □ 3 tbsps water

1. Beat the eggs and the additional egg yolk with the scant ½ cup sugar and the orange flower water.

2. Bring the milk to the boil and beat it into the above mixture. Allow to cool.

3. For the caramel, heat the ½ cup sugar and the water together, stirring continuously until the sugar has dissolved. Increase the heat and boil the mixture, until a light brown caramel is formed.

4. Pour the caramel immediately into the bottom of four ovenproof ramekins. Allow to cool.

5. Pour the cooled egg mixture into the ramekins, filling them to the top. Place them in a rectangular, ovenproof dish and fill the dish with hot water.

6. Cook for 45 minutes in a low oven (300°F). Allow to cool, then turn out before serving.

□ TIME   Preparation takes about 30 minutes and cooking takes approximately 45 minutes.

□ COOK'S TIP   To test for doneness, insert a knife tip into the custards; if it comes out clean, they are cooked.

□ WATCHPOINT   The cooking of the crème caramel should be done slowly, in a low temperature oven, or the egg custard thickens too quickly and becomes spongy.

□

OPPOSITE

ORANGE
FLOWER CRÈME
CARAMEL

MOLDED RICE PUDDING

*Serve these individual puddings with a custard sauce,
flavored with orange flower water and decorated with a little
fruit purée, and watch any preconceptions people may have
about rice pudding being nursery food just disappear.*

Step 2

Step 3

☐ 1 cup long-grain rice   ☐ 2 tbsps raisins   ☐ 6 tbsps sugar   ☐ 5 cups milk   ☐ 2 egg yolks   ☐ ¾ cup heavy cream

1. Rinse and drain the rice.

2. In a saucepan, add the raisins and sugar to the milk, then stir in the rice. Cook over a low heat, stirring often, until the rice has absorbed all the milk and the mixture has thickened.

3. Add the egg yolks and beat continuously over a low heat for 2 more minutes.

4. Remove from the heat, add the cream and mix in well. Divide the mixture between six ramekins and leave to chill in the refrigerator for 2 hours.

5. Turn the puddings out just before serving.

☐ TIME   Preparation takes 20 minutes, plus at least 2 hours chilling time.

☐ VARIATION   The more conventional short-grained rice may also be used for this recipe.

☐

OPPOSITE

MOLDED RICE
PUDDING

—— SERVES 4 ——

RASPBERRY CREAM MOUSSE

The flavor of this lovely summery fruit mousse can be enhanced by adding a tablespoonful of raspberry liqueur to the purée.

Step 4

Step 4

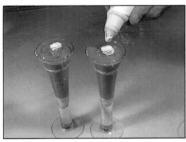

Step 5

☐ 2½-3 cups raspberries, fresh or frozen ☐ ½ cup sugar
☐ 3 egg whites ☐ ½ cup heavy cream ☐ Salt

1. Process the raspberries with 3½ tbsps of the sugar to obtain a purée.

2. Whip the cream until almost stiff, add 1 tbsp of the sugar, then continue whipping until firm. Set aside.

3. Beat the egg whites with a pinch of salt to the soft peak stage, add the remaining 3½ tbsps sugar and continue whipping until the whites are stiff. Fold them into the raspberry purée.

4. Place the whipped cream in a pastry bag and pipe a layer into the bottom of each of four serving dishes/glasses. Fill up with the raspberry mousse, interspersing it with another layer of cream toward the top.

5. If desired, decorate the mousses with a little extra piped whipped cream. Serve immediately.

☐ TIME Preparation takes about 15 minutes.

☐ COOK'S TIP The raspberry pulp can be rubbed through a fine sieve to remove the pips.

☐ WATCHPOINT If using fresh raspberries, add 3 tbsps water to the purée.

☐

OPPOSITE

RASPBERRY
CREAM MOUSSE

─────── SERVES 6 ───────

CARAMEL MOUSSE

*Caramel is one of the simplest and best flavorings for a
mousse that is an instant hit with all who try it.*

Step 3

Step 4

Step 5

───────────────────────────

☐ 4 packages of gelatin   ☐ 5 tbsps sugar   ☐ 2 tbsps water
☐ ½ cup water   ☐ 1⅔ cups custard sauce
☐ ¾ cup whipping cream

───────────────────────────

1. Soften the gelatin in a little cold water.

2. Boil the sugar and the 2 tbsps water to obtain a rich brown caramel. Add the ½ cup water carefully, stirring, and reheating if necessary, to dissolve the caramel. Reserve a little caramel for decorating the mousse.

3. Stir the gelatin into the remaining caramel while this is still hot and mix until the gelatin is completely dissolved.

4. Mix together the custard and the caramel mixture. Chill in the refrigerator until almost set.

5. Whip the cream and fold it gently into the caramel/custard mixture. Pour into a mold or serving dish and leave in the refrigerator for at least 2 hours, until completely set.

6. Unmold if necessary, decorate with the reserved caramel and serve chilled.

☐ TIME   Preparation takes about 30 minutes and cooking takes approximately 10 minutes, plus at least 2 hours chilling time.

☐ COOK'S TIP   The caramel must have dissolved completely before the gelatin is added.

☐ WATCHPOINT   Add the water to the caramel carefully, to avoid splattering.

☐

OPPOSITE

CARAMEL
MOUSSE

———— SERVES 4 ————

BANANA MOUSSE

*This mousse contains no eggs nor is it set with gelatin – the
result is a very creamy confection, perfectly complemented by
its rich chocolate sauce.*

Step 4

Step 4

Step 4

□ ½ cup unsweetened chocolate □ 4 tbsps heavy cream
□ 14 oz peeled bananas □ 2 tbsps sugar
□ 2 tbsps banana liqueur □ ½ lemon □ ½ cup heavy cream

1. Break the chocolate into small pieces. Bring the 4 tbsps cream to a boil in a small pan. Pour the boiling cream over the chocolate and mix until the chocolate has entirely melted and the mixture is smooth. Set aside to cool.

2. Combine the bananas, sugar, banana liqueur and the juice of ½ lemon in a food processor and purée until smooth. Pour the purée into a bowl.

3. Beat the ½ cup heavy cream until stiff. Fold it gently but thoroughly into the banana purée.

4. Divide half the banana mousse between four coupes. Cover with the chocolate sauce. Top with the remaining banana mousse and chill well before serving.

□ TIME   Preparation takes about 15 minutes and cooking takes approximately 3 minutes, plus extra chilling time.

□ SERVING IDEA   Decorate the mousse with melted chocolate and serve with almond tile cookies or macaroons.

□ WATCHPOINT   It is important to add the lemon juice to the banana purée to prevent darkening.

□

OPPOSITE

BANANA
MOUSSE

———— SERVES 6 ————

FRESH FRUIT IN ORANGE JELLY

This fruit dessert looks a treat as well as tasting like one.

Step 4

Step 5

Step 5

☐ 2 cups fresh orange juice ☐ 1 cup fresh grapefruit juice
☐ ¼ cup sugar ☐ 1 tbsp orange liqueur ☐ 2 packages gelatin
☐ 1 kiwi, peeled ☐ 1 orange, peeled ☐ 3 fresh figs
☐ 1 apple, peeled ☐ 1 bunch grapes, seeded

1. Boil the orange and grapefruit juices together with the sugar and liqueur, until the sugar has dissolved.

2. Soften the gelatin in a little water, whip it into the hot juices until dissolved and then allow to cool.

3. Prepare the fruit: cut the kiwi into rounds, the orange into segments, the figs into slices, the apple into cubes and either leave the grapes whole or cut in half.

4. Pour a little of the juice/jelly mixture into the base of a glass dish. Set in the refrigerator for 15 minutes.

5. Place a round of kiwi slices in the centre, then a round of fig slices around the kiwi. Pour over a little more jelly and leave to set in the refrigerator for another 15 minutes.

6. Sprinkle over the cubed apple, pour over enough jelly to cover the apple and leave to set in the refrigerator.

7. Decorate another layer with the orange segments and the grapes. Pour over a little more jelly and leave to set in the refrigerator.

8. Make a final layer using the remaining kiwi slices, pour over the remaining jelly and chill for 24 hours in the refrigerator.

9. To serve, turn the jelly out, by shaking the dish firmly. Serve chilled.

☐ TIME Preparation takes about 2 hours, cooking takes about 5 minutes and 24 hours is required for setting and chilling.

☐ WATCHPOINT To speed up the setting process between each fruit layer, set the jelly in the freezer. Once set, chill for 24 hours in the refrigerator.

☐ VARIATION This jelly can be made with any fresh fruit in season.

☐

OPPOSITE

FRESH FRUIT IN
ORANGE JELLY

STRAWBERRY MOUSSE

*Made with fresh strawberries, this mousse is the very best of
summer desserts; made with frozen strawberries, it's a
welcome reminder of summer's glories.*

Step 2

Step 2

Step 2

□ 1 cup water   □ ⅔ cup sugar
□ 2½ cups fresh or frozen strawberries   □ 2 packages gelatin
□ ½ cup heavy cream   □ 3 tbsps strawberries, diced
□ Strawberry purée and mint leaves, to decorate

1. Boil the water and sugar together for 7 minutes to obtain a light syrup.

2. Add the 2½ cups strawberries and set aside for about 15 minutes. Purée the mixture, then pass the purée through a sieve to eliminate the seeds.

3. Soften the gelatin in a little cold water.

4. Measure out 1 cup of purée, reheat if not hot, then add the gelatin and stir until it has completely dissolved. Add the diced strawberry then set aside until the mixture is cool but not set.

5. Whip the cream until thick. Fold it gently but thoroughly into the cooled strawberry mixture. Pour the mousse into four individual molds or one large mold and leave to set in the refrigerator for at least 2 hours.

6. To serve, unmold the mousses and surround with the strawberry purée and finely shredded mint leaves. Any remaining strawberries/mint leaves can be used to decorate the mousses.

□ TIME   Preparation takes about 35 minutes and cooking takes approximately 10 minutes, plus at least 2 hours setting/chilling time.

□ VARIATION   This recipe works equally well with raspberries, apricots or peaches.

□ BUYING TIP   Use frozen strawberries, partially defrosted, when fresh ones are not in season.

□

OPPOSITE

STRAWBERRY
MOUSSE

—————— SERVES 6 ——————

LIGHT ORANGE MOUSSE

Freshly squeezed orange juice is part of the secret of the tangy taste of this light orange mousse.

Step 1

Step 1

Step 1

☐ ½ orange   ☐ 2 eggs, separated   ☐ 2 tbsps sugar
☐ 2 tsps flour   ☐ 1 cup freshly squeezed orange juice
☐ 2 packages gelatin, softened in cold water   ☐ 3 tbsps sugar
☐ ½ cup heavy cream   ☐ 1 tbsp orange liqueur
☐ Fresh orange segments or candied orange pieces

1. Cut the peel from the ½ orange using a very sharp knife. Cut the peel into very thin strips. Reserve a few strips for decoration, then finely chop the rest into tiny cubes. Blanch the strips and the cubes separately in boiling water for 1 minute, rinse and set aside to drain.

2. Beat together the egg yolks and the 2 tbsps sugar. Add the flour and beat again.

3. Bring the orange juice to a boil. Mix the orange juice into the egg yolk mixture, place back on a gentle heat and stir continuously until the mixture thickens. Stir in the gelatin, heat gently until dissolved, then set aside to cool.

4. Once the orange mixture has cooled but not set, beat the egg whites until foamy. Continue to beat while adding the 3 tbsps sugar gradually until a thick smooth meringue is obtained.

5. Whip the cream until thick.

6. Mix the chopped peel and the orange liqueur into the cooled orange mixture, then delicately fold in first the meringue and then the whipped cream.

7. Turn into either one large mold or six individual molds and leave to set in the refrigerator for at least 3 hours before serving. Decorate with the reserved strips of peel and either fresh orange segments or candied orange pieces.

☐ TIME   Preparation takes about 30 minutes, plus at least 3 hours setting/chilling time.

☐ VARIATION   Try this mousse recipe using other citrus fruits: grapefruit, mandarins, etc.

☐

OPPOSITE

LIGHT ORANGE
MOUSSE

— SERVES 6 —

BLINIS WITH PAPAYA MOUSSE

This dessert is a wonderful combination of flavors and looks spectacular, although it is easy both to make and to assemble.

Step 8

Step 9

Step 10

BLINIS
☐ 1¼ cups all-purpose flour   ☐ 1 tsp yeast
☐ 1 cup milk, scalded and cooled to 85°F   ☐ 1 egg
☐ 4 tsps sugar   ☐ 2 tsps butter

PAPAYA MOUSSE
☐ 1¼ cups papaya flesh, chopped   ☐ 4 tbsps sugar
☐ 2 tbsps water   ☐ 2 packages gelatin
☐ 1¼ cups heavy cream

1. To make the blinis, place half the flour in a bowl. Add the yeast and milk, mix together thoroughly and leave the mixture to rise in a warm place for 2 hours.

2. Add the egg, sugar and remaining flour, mix in well and leave the mixture to rise again in a warm place for 1 hour.

3. Place the papaya flesh in a food processor along with the sugar and water and mix to a pulp.

4. Heat the pulp gently in a saucepan. Soften the gelatin in a little cold water, then mix thoroughly into the hot pulp. Set aside to cool.

5. Cook the blinis in batches, by heating a little nut of the butter in a very small sauté pan. Add a portion of the batter and cook as for pancakes, turning each "pancake" once to cook the other side. Once cooked, leave to cool on a cake rack. Use all the batter in this way.

6. Use a biscuit cutter to cut each "pancake" either into rounds to fit individual molds or into decorative shapes if making one large dish.

7. Whip the cream and fold it gently but thoroughly into the papaya pulp.

8. Either place a blini in the bottom of each of six individual molds or place a layer of blinis in the base of one ring or spring-form mold.

9. Fill the molds or mold almost to the top with the mousse.

10. Cover with a second blini or layer of blinis. Leave to set and chill in the refrigerator for at least 2 hours. Unmold and serve cold.

☐ TIME   Preparation takes about 40 minutes, plus 3 hours rising time, and cooking takes approximately 20 minutes, plus at least 2 hours chilling time.

☐ COOK'S TIP   The pulp could be heated in a microwave oven for speed, before adding the gelatin.

☐ WATCHPOINT   The whipped cream should be added when the pulp is cool but not completely set.

☐

OPPOSITE

BLINIS WITH
PAPAYA MOUSSE

— 104 —

––––––––– SERVES 6 –––––––––

PEAR CHARLOTTE

*This delicately flavored charlotte benefits from being made
using the highest quality canned pears you can afford.*

Step 5

Step 7

Step 8

☐ 1 large can pears in syrup   ☐ 2 tbsps sugar
☐ ½ cup fromage frais   ☐ 2 packages gelatin
☐ 4 tbsps pear liqueur   ☐ 4 tbsps water   ☐ ¾ cup heavy cream
☐ 14 ladyfingers   ☐ Melted chocolate, to decorate

1. Remove one canned pear, cut into dice and set aside. In a food processor, purée the remaining pears with the sugar and ½ cup of the syrup from the can.

2. Mix the pear purée with the fromage frais.

3. Soften the gelatin in a little cold water then place in a saucepan with 2 tbsps of the pear liqueur and 2 tbsps of the water. Stir over a gentle heat to dissolve. Do not allow the gelatin mixture to boil.

4. Mix the dissolved gelatin into the fromage frais and pear mixture.

5. Whip the cream until thick, then fold into the above mixture. Carefully fold in the reserved diced pear.

6. Mix together the remaining 2 tbsps pear liqueur and 2 tbsps water.

7. Brush the ladyfingers with the above mixture, then use them to line the bottom and sides of a charlotte mold or straight-sided bowl.

8. Turn the pear mousse into the lined mold. Leave to set in the refrigerator for at least 3 hours. Turn out and serve chilled, decorated with a little melted chocolate.

☐ TIME   Preparation takes about 30 minutes, plus at least 3 hours setting/chilling time.

☐ WATCHPOINT   Fold the cream and the diced pear very carefully into the mousse mixture to retain as much air and volume as possible.

☐ COOK'S TIP   Add a little color by replacing the diced pear with diced strawberries.

☐ BUYING TIP   If fromage frais is not available, use sieved cottage or Ricotta cheese.

☐

OPPOSITE

PEAR
CHARLOTTE

—— SERVES 6 ——

CLEMENTINE MOUSSE WITH KIWI FRUIT SAUCE

A light, fruity dessert, flavored
with clementine juice. The French call it
'Bavarois aux Clementines, Coulis Kiwi'.

Step 1

Step 1

Step 3

□ 2 cups clementine juice   □ 6 sheets gelatin, pre-soaked
□ 1¾ cups whipping cream   □ ½ cup of sugar
□ 6 kiwi fruit, peeled

1. In a saucepan, bring the clementine juice to the boil and stir in the drained sheets of gelatin. Tip the juice into a large bowl, stir until the gelatin has dissolved and then cool in the refrigerator until it just starts to thicken.

2. Whip the cream and, when it is quite thick, whip in half the sugar.

3. Gently fold the cream into the cooled, thickened fruit juice and pour into 6 custard cups. Put them into the refrigerator to set – this takes 24 hours.

4. Just before serving, peel the kiwi fruit and blend them in a blender with the remaining sugar and 2 tbsps of water, until smooth.

5. Turn out the mousse onto small plates and serve the kiwi fruit mixture poured around.

TIME   Cooking takes about 5 minutes, preparation takes 35 minutes and setting time is at least 24 hours.

COOK'S TIP   To turn out the mousse cleanly, dip the custard cups in boiling water and turn out immediately.

SERVING IDEA   Garnish the plates with a little chopped strawberry and finely chopped mint.

□

OPPOSITE

CLEMENTINE
MOUSSE WITH
KIWI FRUIT SAUCE

SERVES 6

CHESTNUT MOUSSE

*Chestnuts are a favorite European ingredient in sweet dishes
and using shop-bought, sweetened purée greatly shortens the
preparation time without lessening the flavor in any way.*

Step 4

Step 4

Step 4

☐ 1 cup custard sauce
☐ 1¼ cups canned sweetened chestnut purée
☐ 2 packages gelatin
☐ 2 tbsps maraschino, or other sweet liqueur
☐ 1 cup heavy cream   ☐ 4 candied chestnuts, chopped

1. Mix the custard sauce with the chestnut purée.

2. Soften the gelatin in a little cold water. Place in a saucepan with the maraschino and 2 tbsps of water. Heat gently, stirring until the gelatin dissolves.

3. Pour the contents of the saucepan into the chestnut purée mixture, combine well and set aside.

4. While the above is cooling, place the cream in the freezer for 5 minutes and then whip until slightly thickened.

5. Using a spatula, fold the cream into the chestnut mixture. Pour the mousse into the mold of your choice.

6. Leave to set and chill for at least 2 hours in the refrigerator. Turn out and serve decorated with the chopped candied chestnuts.

☐ TIME   Preparation takes about 30 minutes, plus at least 2 hours setting/chilling time.

☐ COOK'S TIP   Freezing the cream for a few minutes ensures greater volume when whipped.

☐ WATCHPOINT   The gelatin must not be allowed to boil during heating.

☐

OPPOSITE

CHESTNUT
MOUSSE

PRUNE AND ARMAGNAC MOUSSE

*Prunes achieve a new sophistication and dinner-party status
in this rich mousse, laced with Armagnac.*

Step 1

Step 3

Step 4

☐ 1 cup fromage frais ☐ 1 cup custard sauce
☐ ¾ cup pitted prunes ☐ 1 sachet gelatin
☐ 2 tbsps Armagnac, or to taste ☐ ½ cup heavy cream

1. Place the fromage frais and the custard sauce in a food processor. Add the prunes and process quickly. Turn the mixture into a bowl.

2. Soften the gelatin in a little cold water then place in a small saucepan with a further 2 tbsps water and the Armagnac. Heat gently and stir until the gelatin dissolves.

3. Pour the gelatin mixture into the fromage frais mixture and beat together well.

4. Whip the cream until light and fluffy, then fold gently into the above.

5. Divide the mousse mixture between four individual molds or ramekins and leave to set in the refrigerator for at least 2 hours.

6. Unmold and serve chilled.

☐ TIME   Preparation takes about 30 minutes, plus a minimum of 2 hours chilling time.

☐ SERVING IDEA   Serve with an Armagnac-flavored custard sauce, to which chopped prunes could be added if desired.

☐ BUYING TIP   Fromage frais can be replaced with sieved cottage or Ricotta cheese.

☐ COOK'S TIP   Use stainless steel molds if possible, as unmolding is then easier.

☐

OPPOSITE

PRUNE AND
ARMAGNAC
MOUSSE

—— SERVES 4 ——

LIME MOUSSE

*Lime juice makes a very refreshing mousse that is beautifully
decorated – a perfect dinner party choice.*

Step 6

Step 7

Step 8

☐ 1½ packages gelatin   ☐ 1 cup lime juice
☐ 1cup warm custard sauce   ☐ Peel of two lemons/limes
☐ 1 cup water   ☐ 2 tbsps sugar
☐ 1½ cups heavy cream

1. Soften 1 package of gelatin in a little cold water.

2. Add first the lime juice and then the softened gelatin to the warm custard sauce and stir well to mix thoroughly. Set aside to cool.

3. Cut the lemon peel into very thin strips and blanch in boiling water, then drain and rinse. Place the peel with ½ cup of water and the 2 tbsps of sugar into a pan and boil on a high heat until a thick syrup is obtained.

4. Soften the remaining ½ package of gelatin in a little cold water. When the lemon peel mixture reaches the thick syrup stage, add the second gelatin mixture and another ½ cup of water. Bring to a boil and set aside to cool.

5. Whip the cream until thick and add to the lime custard. Use a spatula to fold in the cream gently until well blended. Pour into a stainless steel ring mold set on a serving plate and leave to set in the refrigerator for at least 2 hours.

6. When the mousse is set, top with the lemon peel, spreading it evenly over the surface.

7. Spread the lightly set syrup over the top. Leave to set for a further hour or more in the refrigerator before serving.

8. To serve, ease the mousse out of the mold by running the tip of a sharp knife all around the edge.

☐ TIME   Preparation takes about 35 minutes and chilling takes at least 3 hours.

☐ FREEZER TIP   The mousse can be frozen whole; defrost in the refrigerator the day before use.

☐ VARIATION   The limes could be replaced with lemons.

☐ COOK'S TIP   Limes tend to be very hard. If you work them in your fingers for a few minutes, it will be easier to extract the juice.

☐

OPPOSITE

LIME MOUSSE

——— SERVES 4 ———

PASSION FRUIT OMELET

*Sweet omelets make a pleasant change from the more usual
savory variety, and are best served after a light meal, since
they are quite substantial.*

Step 1

Step 2

Step 3

☐ 4 passion fruit   ☐ 12 eggs   ☐ 2 tbsps sugar
☐ 2 tbsps ground coconut   ☐ Oil for greasing

1. Cut the passion fruit in half with a very sharp knife.

2. Place the eggs in a bowl and add the pulp from 2 of the passion fruit.

3. Add the sugar and coconut and beat all the ingredients together well.

4. Heat the oil in a frying pan and, when very hot, pour in the egg mixture. Once the omelet is almost cooked, roll it up in the pan.

5. Serve hot with the remaining passion fruit pulp, sweetened if necessary with a little sugar.

☐ TIME   Preparation takes about 15 minutes and cooking approximately 5 minutes.

☐ SERVING IDEA   Either make one very large omelet or four smaller ones.

☐ WATCHPOINT   The oil must be hot before adding the egg mixture in order to seal the base of the omelet immediately.

☐ BUYING TIP   Look for passion fruit that are wrinkled, as these are usually riper and therefore sweeter.

☐

OPPOSITE

PASSION FRUIT
OMELET

─────── SERVES 6 ───────

COCONUT SOUFFLÉ

*Soufflés always impress; they are actually quite
straightforward to make, but must be brought to the table
direct from the oven – before they sink!*

Step 3

Step 5

Step 5

───────────────────────────

□ 1 cup milk   □ 1½ eggs   □ 4 tbsps sugar
□ 4 tsps shredded coconut   □ 2 tbsps flour   □ 1 egg yolk
□ 2 tbsps coconut liqueur   □ 2 tsps butter
□ 4 tsps powdered sugar   □ 4 egg whites

───────────────────────────

1. To make a pastry cream begin by bringing the milk to a boil. In a bowl, beat together the 1½ eggs, the 4 tbsps sugar, the coconut and the flour.

2. Pour the boiling milk over the egg mixture, stirring continuously, then pour it back into the pan. Bring to a boil, stirring, then remove from the heat and allow to cool.

3. When the cream has cooled, beat in the egg yolk, then stir in the coconut liqueur.

4. Use the butter to grease six ramekins. Sprinkle the insides with the powdered sugar, shaking out any excess.

5. Whip the egg whites until very firm. Fold them gently but thoroughly into the pastry cream.

6. Fill the ramekins three-quarters full with the soufflé mixture. Bake in a hot oven (400°F) for about 20-30 minutes, until well risen and firm. Serve immediately.

□ TIME   Preparation takes about 30 minutes and cooking takes 20-30 minutes.

□ VARIATION   The flavor can be varied by using different flavored alcohols or liqueurs.

□ BUYING TIP   Both fresh and packaged coconut are suitable for this recipe.

□

OPPOSITE

COCONUT
SOUFFLÉ

PEAR OMELET

The addition of a small amount of ground cloves to this sweet omelet gives it a very special flavor that marries particularly well with the pears.

Step 3

Step 4

Step 5

□ 4-5 pears in syrup   □ 12 eggs   □ 2 tbsps heavy cream
□ 2 tbsps sugar   □ 1 whole clove   □ Oil or butter

1. Cut the pears into small, even-sized cubes.

2. Beat the eggs with the cream and sugar. Finely grind about one eighth of the clove into the mixture. Stir in the pears.

3. Heat approximately 2 tbsps of oil or butter in an omelet pan. When hot, pour in the egg mixture

4. Stir the mixture a little in the pan, then cook for a few minutes until set.

5. Shake the omelet loose and flip it over, as for a pancake, and cook on the other side. Serve warm.

□ TIME   Preparation takes about 20 minutes and cooking takes 6-10 minutes.

□ COOK'S TIP   Instead of flipping the omelet over, slide it onto a large serving plate, replace the pan upside down over the plate and then turn it the right way up.

□ VARIATION   Using a small pan, the egg mixture could be divided to make four individual omelets.

□

OPPOSITE

PEAR OMELET

—— SERVES 4 ——

CHILLED SOUFFLÉS GRAND MARNIER

A dessert from the classic repertoire that looks impressive and tastes even better.

☐ 6 egg yolks   ☐ ½ cup sugar   ☐ 3 tbsps Grand Marnier
☐ 6 egg whites   ☐ ¾ cup whipping cream

Step 1

Step 1

Step 5

1. Prepare four ramekins: fix a "collar" of waxed paper around each one, securing the paper with Scotch tape.

2. Place the egg yolks, sugar, Grand Marnier and 1 tbsp of water in a bowl set over a saucepan of simmering water and beat until the mixture forms a ribbon, or thick thread, if dropped from a spoon. Remove from the heat and continue to beat until the mixture has cooled.

3. Whip the egg whites until stiff peaks form. Whip the cream until light and fluffy.

4. Fold the egg whites gently into the egg mixture, so as not to lose any of the volume, and then fold in the whipped cream.

5. When the mixture is evenly mixed together divide it equally between the prepared ramekins. Leave to chill in the refrigerator for at least 3 hours, or until set. Remove the paper collars from the ramekins just before serving.

☐ TIME   Preparation takes about 40 minutes, plus at least 3 hours chilling time.

☐ VARIATION   Different liqueurs can be used to vary the flavor of the soufflés.

☐

OPPOSITE

CHILLED
SOUFFLÉS
GRAND
MARNIER

APPLE OMELET

*Calvados is a fiery apple brandy from Normandy in France,
and this sweet omelet is just one of the many regional recipes
that make the most of its fruity nature.*

Step 2

Step 4

□ 2 apples   □ 12 eggs   □ 4 tbsps sugar
□ 1 tbsp Calvados   □ 3 tbsps butter   □ 2 tbsps raisins

1. Peel and core the apples and cut them into thick slices.

2. Beat the eggs with the sugar and Calvados.

3. Melt half the butter in a frying pan. When hot, sauté the apple with the raisins until the apples are lightly browned. Remove from the heat.

4. Heat a little butter in a small sauté or omelet pan. When hot, pour in a quarter of the omelet mixture, mix a little, then add a quarter of the apple mixture, pushing it well into the omelet.

5. When one side is cooked, turn the omelet over to cook the other side. Serve immediately. Repeat the procedure until all four omelets have been cooked. If preferred, the egg and apple mixtures could be used to make one large omelet.

□ TIME   Preparation takes about 10 minutes and cooking takes approximately 5 minutes.

□ COOK'S TIP   If less time is available, dice the apple, sauté as above then beat into the egg mixture and cook as for an ordinary omelet.

□ VARIATION   Reserve the Calvados and use it to flambé the cooked omelet, heating the liqueur slightly before pouring it over the omelet.

□

OPPOSITE

APPLE OMELET

SERVES 4

PEACH MELBA

*Homemade vanilla ice cream lifts this famous dessert into
the super-class.*

Step 1

Step 2

Step 3

Step 4

□ 6 egg yolks   □ ½ cup sugar   □ 2 cups milk
□ ½ vanilla bean   □ 2 cups raspberries   □ 1 tbsp sugar
□ 2 tsps kirsch   □ 4 peaches

1. Make a custard base by beating together the egg yolks and sugar. Bring the milk to a boil with the vanilla bean.

2. Pour the scalded milk over the egg yolk mixture, beating rapidly.

3. Return the mixture to the saucepan and stir continuously over a gentle heat until thick.

4. Remove from heat when the custard coats the back of the spoon. Pour into a clean bowl and allow to cool.

5. Crush the raspberries with the sugar and kirsch.

6. Place the cooled custard in an ice-cream maker and process according to the manufacturer's directions. Place in the freezer until firm. Alternatively, pour the cooled custard into a rigid freezer container and freeze for 2-2½ hours until mushy. Remove from the freezer, turn into a bowl and beat well. Return to the container and freeze until firm.

7. Cut the peaches into even slices.

8. Spread the crushed raspberries over the bottom of four plates. Spread out the peach slices and top with a ball of vanilla ice cream. Serve immediately.

□ TIME   Preparation takes about 30 minutes, cooking takes approximately 10 minutes, freezing the ice cream using an ice-cream maker takes about 45 minutes, longer in a freezer.

□ WATCHPOINT   Cooking the custard should be done slowly over a very gentle heat to prevent it curdling.

□ COOK'S TIP   The vanilla bean can be used as is, or it may be split and the seeds scraped out and added to the milk.

□

OPPOSITE

PEACH MELBA

—— SERVES 6 ——

FROZEN NOUGAT

This dream of a dessert is extremely rich and filling, so a little goes a long way!

Step 2

Step 3

Step 4

Step 5

☐ ½ cup raisins   ☐ ½ cup candied fruit
☐ 2 tbsps coconut liqueur   ☐ ½ cup honey   ☐ 4 tsps sugar
☐ 2 tbsps water   ☐ 4 egg whites
☐ ¾ cup heavy cream   ☐ 2 tbsps crushed praliné

1. Leave the raisins and the candied fruit to marinate in the coconut liqueur. Boil the honey, sugar and water in a small saucepan for 3-4 minutes to obtain a thick syrup.

2. Beat the egg whites until very stiff. Add the hot syrup gradually to the egg whites, beating continuously until a thick, smooth meringue is obtaïned.

3. Whip the cream and fold it gently into the meringue mixture.

4. Add the crushed praliné and the raisins and candied fruit together with their marinade; stir in gently.

5. Line a loaf pan with greased wax paper, pour in the nougat mixture and put in the freezer for 24 hours.

6. To serve, turn the frozen nougat out of the loaf pan, remove the wax paper and cut the nougat into wedges or slices. Serve immediately.

☐ TIME   Preparation takes about 40 minutes, plus 24 hours freezing time.

☐ SERVING IDEA   Serve with either a custard sauce or a fresh fruit purée.

☐ COOK'S TIP   When adding the hot syrup to the egg whites, the mixture must be beaten continuously.

☐ WATCHPOINT   Lining the loaf pan makes the frozen nougat easier to turn out.

☐

OPPOSITE

FROZEN
NOUGAT

—— SERVES 4 ——

YOGURT ICE CREAM

This simple-to-make ice cream is an unqualified hit with all who taste it – make plenty, as everyone will come back for more.

Step 4

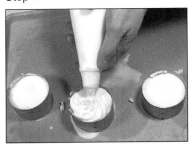
Step 4

☐ ¼ vanilla bean   ☐ 2 cups custard sauce
☐ 1½ cups plain yogurt
☐ Custard sauce, flavored with a little coffee powder

1. Slice open the vanilla bean and remove the seeds by scraping the back of a knife down the inside of the bean.

2. Mix together the custard, yogurt and vanilla seeds, reserving a few seeds for decoration.

3. Place in an ice-cream maker and process according to the manufacturer's instructions for 1 hour, or until set. If an ice-cream maker is not available, put the ice cream mixture into a freezer tray, freeze for about 2 hours, then remove from the freezer, beat the mixture well and return to the freezer until set.

4. Fill four individual metal rings or molds with the ice cream, piping any remaining mixture decoratively over the top and set in the freezer for 5 minutes.

5. To serve, unmold the ice cream, decorate with the remaining vanilla seeds and serve with the coffee-flavored custard sauce.

☐ TIME   Preparation takes about 20 minutes, plus freezing time, which will depend on the method used.

☐ SERVING IDEA   The ice cream could also be served in little balls.

☐ COOK'S TIP   Freeze the molds or rings before use. This helps prevent the ice-cream from melting.

☐ WATCHPOINT   Decoration and serving of the ice cream should be done very quickly.

☐

OPPOSITE

YOGURT ICE
CREAM

CHOUX PUFFS WITH CARAMEL ICE CREAM

A variation on the profiteroles theme that substitutes ice cream for the more usual whipped cream filling in the choux puffs.

Step 6

Step 6

Step 6

□ ½ cup sugar □ 2 tbsps water □ ½ cup water
□ 1 cup custard sauce □ 2 tbsps butter □ ½ cup water
□ 1 tsp sugar □ Pinch of salt □ ½ cup all-purpose flour
□ 2 eggs

---

1. Make a caramel using the ½ cup sugar and the 2 tbsps water. When the sugar has caramelized, pour in one ½ cup water, place back on the heat for 1 minute and stir to dissolve, then set aside to cool.

2. Combine the cooled caramel with the custard sauce, stirring together thoroughly, then pour into an ice-cream maker and process until the ice cream sets. Alternatively, pour the mixture into a freezing tray and freeze for 2 hours. Remove from the freezer, thoroughly beat the part-frozen mixture and then replace in the freezer until set.

3. To make the choux paste, bring the butter, the remaining water and sugar and the salt to a boil.

4. When the mixture is boiling, tip in all the flour at once, mix in thoroughly and cook the paste, stirring continuously, for another 2 minutes.

5. Remove the paste from the heat, add the first egg and beat until really well mixed in. Add the second egg, beating well to obtain a smooth, elastic dough.

6. Place the paste in a pastry bag with a plain metal tip. Pipe balls of choux paste onto a greased cookie sheet. Dip a fork in beaten egg and slightly flatten each of the balls. Bake in a hot oven (400°F) for about 20 minutes, or until lightly browned and well puffed. Remove from the oven and set aside to cool.

7. Cut open the base of each choux puff and spoon in a little of the caramel ice cream. Chill the filled puffs for 30 minutes in the freezer before serving.

□ TIME Preparation takes about 1 hour, plus at least one hour to make the ice cream, and cooking takes 15-20 minutes.

□ SERVING IDEA Make a little extra caramel and pour it over the choux balls before serving, or serve with a custard sauce, sprinkled with crushed praliné.

□ WATCHPOINT The choux balls must not be removed from the oven until they are completely cooked, i.e. lightly browned and well puffed.

□ COOK'S TIP If you make your own custard sauce for the ice cream, do not make it too sweet as the caramel sweetens it considerably.

□

OPPOSITE

CHOUX PUFFS
WITH CARAMEL
ICE CREAM

—— SERVES 4 ——

PEARS "BELLE HÉLÈNE"

Ice cream desserts are always popular and this classic combination is no exception.

Step 1

Step 1

Step 2

☐ 4 canned pears in syrup   ☐ ½ cup cooking chocolate
☐ ½ cup milk   ☐ 2 tsps sugar   ☐ 1-1½ cups vanilla ice cream
☐ 1 tbsp toasted, slivered almonds

1. Cut the pears in half lengthwise and remove all the seeds from the center with a melon baller.

2. Cut each half pear into even slices.

3. Melt the chocolate with the milk and sugar in a bowl set over a saucepan of boiling water. Mix together well.

4. Fan out each pear on a serving plate. Pour the chocolate sauce around the edges, top with a ball of ice cream and sprinkle over the almonds. Serve immediately.

☐ TIME   Preparation takes about 15 minutes.

☐ SERVING IDEA   Serve in parfait glasses instead of on plates.

☐ COOK'S TIP   Flavor the chocolate sauce with 1 tbsp of rum and a few raisins.

☐ VARIATION   Use fresh pears and poach them in a light sugar syrup.

☐

OPPOSITE

PEARS "BELLE
HÉLÈNE"

CARAMELIZED TARTE TATIN

This classic French dessert is one of the tastiest ways of serving apples.

Step 2

Step 3

Step 5

□ 4 large apples   □ ¾ cup sugar   □ ¼ cup butter
□ 3 cups puff paste   □ Cinnamon

1. Peel, core and quarter the apples.

2. Sprinkle a flameproof/ovenproof pan with sugar and dot with butter. Caramelize over a high heat, then remove from the heat to cool.

3. Distribute the apple quarters evenly in the caramel.

4. Roll the paste into a round, slightly larger than the pan.

5. Sprinkle cinnamon, to taste, over the apple quarters and place the paste on top. Tuck the edges down over the apple quarters, so that the tart is sealed all around the edge.

6. Bake in a preheated, hot oven (400°F) for approximately 20 minutes.

7. Allow the tart to cool for 10 minutes, then turn out onto a serving plate and serve immediately.

□ TIME   Preparation takes about 20 minutes and cooking also takes approximately 20 minutes.

□ SERVING IDEA   Serve the tart with whipped heavy cream or cinnamon-flavored ice cream.

□ WATCHPOINT   Do not allow the caramel to burn; turn the heat off as soon as the sugar mixture turns light brown.

□ COOK'S TIP   If you do not turn the tart out within 10 minutes, reheat over a high heat for 2 minutes.

□

OPPOSITE

CARAMELIZED
TARTE TATIN

—— SERVES 4 ——

STRAWBERRY TARTS

*Using an almond-flavored cream in these little tartlets
instead of ordinary pastry cream complements the flavor of
the strawberries perfectly.*

Step 5

Step 7

Step 8

DOUGH
☐ 1 cup all-purpose flour ☐ ¼ cup sugar ☐ ½ egg yolk
☐ 2 tbsps water ☐ Pinch salt ☐ ¼ cup butter, softened

ALMOND CREAM
☐ Scant ½ cup butter, softened ☐ Scant ½ cup sugar
☐ ½ cup ground almonds ☐ 1 egg

TOPPING
☐ 3 cups strawberries, hulled and washed
☐ 3 tbsps strawberry glaze, or melted strawberry jam

1. To make the dough, mix together the first five ingredients. Add the softened butter, mix thoroughly and form into a ball. Allow to rest in the refrigerator.

2. Make the almond cream by beating together the butter and sugar until light. Add the ground almonds and the egg, mix well and set aside in the refrigerator.

3. Dry the strawberries. Trim as necessary and slice neatly.

4. Roll out the dough and use to line four individual non-stick pie pans, or one large one if preferred. Prick the bases with a fork.

5. Either use a pastry bag to pipe the almond cream into the tart cases or simply spoon in the cream and spread it evenly with the back of the spoon.

6. Cook in a hot oven (400°F) for 20 minutes.

7. When the cases are cooked, allow them to cool and then arrange the strawberries decoratively over the cream.

8. Brush the strawberries with the glaze, leave them to set for 30 minutes in the refrigerator and serve chilled.

☐ TIME   Preparation takes 1 hour and cooking takes approximately 20 minutes.

☐ BUYING TIP   Use frozen strawberries when fresh are not in season. Defrost thoroughly and add a little sugar.

☐ WATCHPOINT   It is important to prick the dough before baking to prevent it bubbling up.

☐

OPPOSITE

STRAWBERRY

TARTS

SERVES 4

LEMON TART

*A rich, sweet dough encloses a lemon-flavored filling in this
tangy tart that tastes good any time.*

Step 3

Step 3

Step 5

DOUGH
□ 1¼ cups all-purpose flour   □ ½ egg yolk   □ 4 tsps sugar
□ Pinch salt   □ 2 tbsps water   □ Scant ½ cup butter, softened

FILLING
□ Scant ½ cup butter   □ ½ cup sugar   □ 5 eggs
□ ¾ cup lemon juice, freshly squeezed

1. Place the flour on a work surface or in a bowl and, using your fingertips, gradually work in the ½ egg yolk, sugar, salt and water. Add the softened butter, and work the dough into a ball. Chill for 30 minutes in the refrigerator.

2. Roll the pastry out on a lightly floured surface. Place in a buttered pie pan. Prick with a fork and cover with aluminum foil. Weigh down with a handful of cooking beans. Cook for 20 minutes in a moderate oven (350°F).

3. Meanwhile, place the filling ingredients in a saucepan over a gentle heat, whipping continuously until the mixture thickens. Set aside to cool.

4. When the pie shell is cooked, remove the aluminum foil and the beans. Set aside to cool.

5. When the pie shell is cool, spread the filling evenly inside. Chill for at least 2 hours before serving.

□ TIME   Preparation takes about 30 minutes, plus 30 minutes chilling time, and cooking also takes approximately 30 minutes.

□ SERVING IDEA   Slices of candied lemon can be used to decorate the tart. Brush the surface with a light syrup to make it shiny.

□ VARIATION   When available, limes can be used instead of lemons.

□ WATCHPOINT   While the lemon filling is cooking, stir it continuously, otherwise it will become lumpy.

□

OPPOSITE

LEMON TART

—— SERVES 4 ——

AMANDINES

These rich tartlets are comforting winter fare.

□ 2 cups sweet pie dough   □ 4 tbsps soft butter
□ 4 tbsps sugar   □ 1 egg   □ ⅔ cup ground almonds
□ 2 tbsps raspberry jam

Step 2

Step 3

Step 4

1. Roll the dough out and use to line four individual, greased pie pans. Set aside in the refrigerator.

2. Beat the butter and sugar together until light.

3. Add the egg to the above and continue to beat until completely mixed together.

4. Stir in the ground almonds to form a thick paste.

5. Spread the jam evenly over the base of the four pie shells.

6. Spoon the almond mixture carefully and evenly over the jam, or use a pastry bag to pipe it in. Do not overfill the pie shells.

7. Bake the amandines in a moderate oven (350°F) for about 30 minutes. Allow to cool before removing from the pans.

□ TIME   Preparation takes about 40 minutes and cooking takes approximately 30 minutes.

□ COOK'S TIP   If the almond filling browns too quickly, cover it with a sheet of aluminum foil.

□ WATCHPOINT   The butter should be very soft so that it blends well.

□ VARIATION   A different flavored jam could be used to replace the raspberry.

□

OPPOSITE

AMANDINES

—— SERVES 4 ——

APPLE PIES

*Baking the pies in individual portions gives an elegant touch
to a homely favorite.*

Step 1

Step 3

Step 4

Step 5

☐ 2½ cups basic pie dough   ☐ Flour   ☐ 4 apples
☐ ¼ cup sugar   ☐ Cinnamon   ☐ 1 egg, beaten
☐ Heavy cream, to serve

---

1. Roll out the dough thinly on a floured surface. Cut out eight equal rounds and use four of them to line four individual pie rings or pans.

2. Peel, core and dice the apples. Add the sugar and cinnamon to taste.

3. Fill each of the lined rings generously with apple.

4. Brush the edges of the dough with a little of the beaten egg. Cover each pie with a second dough round, sealing the edges by pinching together firmly. Trim away any excess dough.

5. Brush the top of each pie with beaten egg to give a glossy finish to the pie crust. Bake in a hot oven (400°F) for about 30 minutes, or until golden brown.

6. Serve the pies hot from the oven, accompanied by heavy cream.

☐ TIME   Preparation takes about 40 minutes and cooking takes approximately 30 minutes.

☐ COOK'S TIP   Use any trimmings to decorate the pies, sticking the decorations on with water before covering the pies.

☐

OPPOSITE

APPLE PIES

CARAMELIZED PEAR TARTS

*Pears make a tasty change from apples in these
mouthwatering individual tarts, that are akin to the classic
French Tarte Tatin.*

Step 3

Step 3

☐ 2½ cups puff paste, homemade or shop bought   ☐ 4 pears
☐ 3 tbsps sugar   ☐ 3 tbsps butter, melted

1. Roll out the dough and, using a small plate as a pattern, cut out four equal rounds. Place these on a dampened, non-stick baking sheet.

2. Peel and core the pears. Halve each pear and then slice thinly.

3. Arrange the slices of pear neatly on the pastry rounds. Brush the pear slices with the melted butter.

4. Cook in a hot oven (400°F) for about 15 minutes. When the tarts are almost cooked, remove and sprinkle with sugar. Place them under a hot broiler until caramelized. Serve the tarts warm.

☐ TIME   Preparation takes about 35 minutes and cooking takes approximately 15 minutes.

☐ SERVING IDEA   Serve with caramel-flavored ice cream.

☐ COOK'S TIP   Finely grate a little clove over the top of the tarts to add extra depth of flavor.

☐ WATCHPOINT   Prick the puff paste all over with a fork before arranging the pear on top.

☐

OPPOSITE

CARAMELIZED
PEAR TARTS

—— SERVES 6 ——

WALNUT AND HAZELNUT TART

A variation on the well-known English dessert Bakewell Pudding, this pie is filling and is best served after a light main course.

Step 1

Step 1

Step 2

Step 2

☐ 2 cups pastry dough   ☐ 3 eggs, separated   ☐ ¾ cup sugar
☐ ⅓ cup ground hazelnuts   ☐ ⅓ cup ground walnuts
☐ 3 tbsps raspberry jam

1. Roll out the dough and use to line a 9-inch buttered pie pan, pressing the dough well into the base and sides.

2. Run a rolling pin over the edge of the pan to remove excess dough. Set aside to rest in a cool place.

3. Beat together the egg yolks and the sugar, until light in color. Add the ground nuts and mix thoroughly.

4. Whisk the egg whites until stiff, and gently fold into the above mixture.

5. Spread the jam over the base of the dough and then pour over the nut mixture.

6. Bake in a moderate oven (350°F) for approximately 35 minutes. Allow to cool a little before serving. This tart can also be served cold.

☐ TIME   Preparation takes about 35 minutes and cooking also takes about 35 minutes.

☐ VARIATION   A single type of nut – hazelnut, walnut or almond – could be used.

☐ COOK'S TIP   Grind the nuts yourself using a food processor.

☐

OPPOSITE

WALNUT AND
HAZELNUT TART

─── SERVES 4 ───

PINEAPPLE AND KIWI TART

This fresh fruit tart uses homemade puff paste, but shop-bought could be used if time is short.

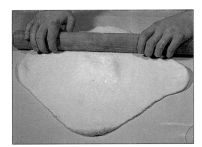

Step 2

Step 3

Step 4

Step 5

□

OPPOSITE

PINEAPPLE AND
KIWI TART

□ 1½ cups all-purpose flour   □ ¼ tsp salt   □ ⅓ cup water
□ ½ cup butter   □ 4 slices fresh pineapple   □ 2 kiwis
□ 1 egg, beaten   □ 1 tsp rum   □ 4 tbsps pastry cream

1. Mix the flour and salt together with enough water to form a slightly elastic dough. Form into an oblong and set aside for 10 minutes.

2. Roll out the four sides of the dough, leaving a slight mound in the center.

3. Place the butter on the mound in the center of the dough and fold each of the four sides over it.

4. Tap the dough down and form it into a square.

5. Roll out the dough into a rectangle. Fold one end into the center, fold in the other end over the first and give the dough a quarter turn to the right. Place in the refrigerator for 10 minutes.

6. Take the dough out of the refrigerator and repeat Step 5 twice more. Place in the refrigerator for a further 10 minutes.

7. Remove from the refrigerator and repeat Step 5 twice more. Place in the refrigerator for a further 10 minutes before use.

8. Cut the pineapple into small chunks or slices and the kiwi into rounds.

9. Roll the dough out very thinly into a large rectangle. Trim the edges and roll out the trimmings to form long strips. Brush the strips with beaten egg and fix to the edges of the puff paste rectangle. Brush the tops of the strips with the remaining beaten egg.

10. Bake in a hot oven (400°F) for approximately 15 minutes. Leave to cool completely after cooking.

11. Mix the rum into the pastry cream, or custard, and spread over the cooked pie shell. Distribute the fruit attractively over the cream.

12. If desired, brush a little white corn syrup over the fruit to make it shine.

□ TIME   Preparation takes about 2 hours and cooking takes approximately 15 minutes.

□ FREEZER TIP   The uncooked pastry can be frozen; defrost well before use.

□ COOK'S TIP   The puff paste must be rolled out evenly so that it rises evenly on cooking.

□ WATCHPOINT   When preparing the puff paste, work on a well-floured surface and use plenty of flour on your rolling pin.

—— SERVES 4 ——

BLUEBERRY TARTS

An all-American favorite baked in small pie pans for individual appeal.

Step 2

Step 3

Step 3

Step 4

☐

OPPOSITE

BLUEBERRY

TARTS

☐ 1¼ cups all-purpose flour   ☐ ½ egg yolk   ☐ pinch salt
☐ 4 tsps sugar   ☐ 2 tbsps water   ☐ 4 tbsps butter, softened
☐ ½ tbsp blueberry liqueur   ☐ 4 tbsps pastry cream
☐ 4 tsps sugar
☐ 3 cups blueberries, frozen or fresh   ☐ ½ tbsp heavy cream
☐ Butter for greasing

1. To make the dough, place the flour on a work surface, or in a bowl, and add the ½ egg yolk, salt and sugar.

2. Add the water drop by drop, and work the ingredients together using your fingertips.

3. Add the softened butter and continue mixing together to form a dough.

4. Work the dough together to form a ball, then chill for 30 minutes in the refrigerator.

5. Mix the liqueur into the pastry cream and blend until smooth.

6. Roll the pastry out on a lightly floured surface. Cut to fit four individual tart pans. Prick the pastry with a fork, cover with aluminum foil and weigh down with a few cooking beans. Bake in a hot oven (400°F) for 20 minutes.

7. Sprinkle the sugar over the blueberries. Stir them from time to time.

8. When the pie shells are cooked, remove the cooking beans and aluminum foil and set the shells aside to cool.

9. When cool, spread a little pastry cream into the base of each shell and top with the sweetened blueberries.

☐ TIME   Preparation takes about 30 minutes, plus 30 minutes chilling time, and cooking takes approximately 20 minutes.

☐ SERVING IDEA   Serve decorated with the cream.

☐ VARIATION   The pastry cream can be flavored with a different liqueur.

☐ COOK'S TIP   If you are using fresh blueberries, add a little more sugar than for frozen ones.

—— SERVES 4 ——

CHEESECAKE

*This simplest of Continental-style cooked cheesecakes is
extra-delicious served with a fresh fruit sauce or purée.*

Step 4

Step 5

□ 2½ cups basic pie dough   □ 1 cup fromage frais
□ 2 eggs, separated   □ ½ cup all-purpose flour
□ ½ cup heavy cream   □ 4 tsps sugar   □ ½ cup honey

1. Roll out the dough and use to line a pie pan.

2. Beat the fromage frais with the egg yolks and the flour, until thoroughly mixed.

3. Add the cream and mix again.

4. Whip the egg whites until firm. Add the sugar gradually, beating continuously until stiff peaks form. Fold the egg whites into the cheese and cream mixture.

5. Fill the pie crust with the cheesecake mixture, which should come up to the very top.

6. Bake in a moderate oven (350°F) for about 30 minutes.

7. Remove the cooked cheesecake from the oven and allow to cool completely before serving.

□ TIME   Preparation takes about 40 minutes and cooking takes approximately 30 minutes.

□ WATCHPOINT   The filling puffs up during cooking, but falls again as the cheesecake cools.

□ COOK'S TIP   The honey may be replaced with sugar if preferred, and sieved cottage or Ricotta cheese can be used in place of the fromage frais.

□

OPPOSITE

CHEESECAKE

—— SERVES 4 ——

CARAMELIZED ORANGE TART

Caramel oranges are a popular and refreshing European dessert; this recipe uses the same idea as the basis of a mouthwatering tart that is even more heavenly served with whipped cream or ice cream.

Step 3

Step 4

☐ ⅔ cup sugar   ☐ 3 tbsps butter   ☐ 3 oranges
☐ 1 unpeeled slice of orange
☐ 12 oz puff paste, homemade or shop bought

1. Make a caramel by boiling the sugar and butter together in an ovenproof frying pan. Allow to cool in the pan.

2. Peel and section the oranges, peeling away the membranes from each segment.

3. Arrange the orange segments around the edge of the pan in a circle on top of the hardened caramel. Place the unpeeled slice of orange in the center.

4. Roll out the dough into a circle to fit the pan. Place the circle of dough over the oranges, pressing it down slightly, then press the dough down well all around the edge of the pan to seal in the oranges and caramel.

5. Cook in a hot oven (400°F) for 15-20 minutes until the pastry is golden brown. Remove the cooked tart from the oven and turn out onto a serving plate, so the caramelized oranges are uppermost. Serve immediately.

☐ TIME   Preparation takes about 15 minutes and cooking takes approximately 20 minutes.

☐ WATCHPOINT   It is important to use an ovenproof frying pan. Beware of spitting caramel when turning out the tart.

☐ COOK'S TIP   Add 1 tbsp of orange liqueur to the caramel for extra flavor.

☐

OPPOSITE

CARAMELIZED
ORANGE TART

--------- SERVES 4 ---------

EXOTIC FRUIT TARTS

These fruit tarts are as delicious served as tea- or coffee-time
treats as they are served for dessert.

Step 3

Step 3

Step 3

□ 2 cups basic pie dough   □ 4 tbsps pastry cream
□ 1 tsp coconut liqueur   □ 1 mango   □ 4 litchis   □ 1 kiwi
□ 8 strawberries   □ 2 figs   □ 1 passion fruit   □ 1 orange
□ Small bunch of grapes

---

1. Roll out the dough and use to line four individual non-stick pie pans. Bake 'blind' (lined with aluminum foil) in a preheated 450°F oven for 10-12 minutes, or until lightly browned, and then allow to cool.

2. Whip the liqueur into the pastry cream.

3. Prepare the fruit by peeling, if necessary, and cutting into attractive shapes.

4. Spread the pastry cream into the bottom of the four cooked, cooled pie shells.

5. Arrange the fruit attractively over the pastry cream and serve.

□ TIME   Preparation takes about 45 minutes and cooking takes approximately 20 minutes.

□ COOK'S TIP   The tarts may be glazed with a little syrup.

□ VARIATION   Depending on the season, use different types of fruit: grenadine, fresh coconut, rambutans.

□

OPPOSITE

EXOTIC FRUIT
TARTS

PARIS-BREST

*This choux paste confection is a traditional French pastry
that would enhance any dinner party. A few chopped
strawberries, in season, could be added to the cream filling
for a delicious variation.*

Step 1

Step 2

Step 2

Step 3

□

OPPOSITE

PARIS-BREST

CHOUX PASTE

□ ½ cup water   □ 2 tbsps butter   □ 1 tsp sugar
□ Salt   □ 4 tbsps flour   □ 2 eggs   □ 1 egg, beaten
□ 1 tbsp slivered almonds   □ Confectioners' sugar

FILLING

□ ¾ cup heavy cream   □ 4 tbsps crushed praliné
□ 4 tbsps pastry cream

1. Place the water, butter, sugar and 2 pinches salt in a saucepan to boil. When the butter has melted and the water is boiling, add the flour all at once. Beat continuously for a few minutes until the dough comes away cleanly from the sides of the pan and forms a ball.

2. Remove the pan from the heat and beat in the eggs one by one, to obtain a smooth choux paste.

3. Place the paste in a pastry bag and pipe out rings onto a non-stick or greased baking sheet. Brush the tops with beaten egg and sprinkle with the almonds. Bake for 20 minutes in a hot oven (400°F) until golden brown. Remove the choux rings from the oven, allow them to cool and then slice them in half horizontally.

4. To make the filling, whip the cream until stiff. Add the praliné to the pastry cream, then fold in the whipped cream. Place the filling in a pastry bag with a plain metal tip.

5. Pipe the filling into the bottom halves of the choux rings. Replace the tops. Sift confectioners' sugar over the pastries and serve immediately.

□ TIME   Preparation takes about 35 minutes and cooking takes approximately 20 minutes.

□ WATCHPOINT   It is important that the choux rings are properly cooked before being removed from the oven, or they will fall apart.

□ COOK'S TIP   When you add the first egg to the choux paste, this will separate, but continue beating and it will become smooth again.

□ BUYING TIP   Praliné is a hazelnut brittle which is available from specialty food shops.

---------- SERVES 4 ----------

KOUIGN AMAN

This rich pastry is traditionally sliced and served warm with coffee.

Step 1

Step 2

☐ 3 cups all-purpose flour   ☐ 1½ tbsps fresh yeast
☐ 1 cup warm water   ☐ ¾ cup butter, at room temperature
☐ ½ cup sugar   ☐ Flour for dredging
---

1. Place the flour in a mound on a work surface or in a bowl. Crumble in the fresh yeast and add the water little by little, working with your fingers to form the ingredients into a dough.

2. When all the ingredients have been worked together, knead the dough for a few minutes, then form it into a ball, and set it aside to rise in a warm place for approximately 1 hour 30 minutes.

3. When the dough has risen, roll it out into a square, leaving a slight mound in the center.

4. Place the butter in the center, flattening it down slightly. Place the sugar on the butter and fold in each of the four sides.

5. Roll the dough out on a well-floured surface to form a long rectangle. Fold one end into the center and fold the other end in over the first.

6. Give the dough a quarter turn and then repeat Step 5. Place the dough in the refrigerator for 10 minutes.

7. After 10 minutes, repeat Step 5 a third time.

8. Form the dough into a round and place on a non-stick cookie sheet. Bake in a hot oven (400°F) for approximately 40 minutes.

9. Leave the cooked Kouign Aman to rest slightly and serve while still warm.

☐ TIME   Preparation takes about 40 minutes, plus a total of 2 hours 10 minutes resting time, and cooking takes approximately 40 minutes.

☐ COOK'S TIP   The Kouign Aman is prepared in the same way as puff paste, except that only three turns are necessary.

☐ WATCHPOINT   On the third turn the butter tends to "sweat"; keep the work surface well floured and cook the finished dough immediately.

☐

OPPOSITE

KOUIGN AMAN

FRESH FRUIT PASTRIES

Fresh fruit combines beautifully with pastry cream and puff paste to make these delectable pastries – they taste even better served with a lightly sweetened raspberry or passion fruit purée.

Step 1

Step 1

□ 1 lb puff paste □ 1 egg, beaten □ 6 tbsps pastry cream
□ 1 kiwi □ 1 orange □ 2 fresh figs □ 2 slices pineapple
□ 1 small bunch grapes □ 1 banana

1. Roll out the dough, and cut it into four rectangles, or other shapes. Place these on a dampened cookie sheet and brush each one with a little beaten egg.

2. Cook in a hot oven (400°F) for 15-20 minutes, until the dough is well risen and golden brown. Remove from the oven and allow to cool.

3. Cut each shape in half and spread 1½ tbsps pastry cream over each bottom half.

4. Prepare the fruit as necessary, trimming and slicing or dicing as desired. Distribute the fruit evenly over the pastry cream and finish each pastry with the four top halves.

□ TIME   Preparation takes 25 minutes and cooking takes approximately 15 minutes.

□ COOK'S TIP   The dough must be rolled out evenly so that it rises uniformly on cooking.

□ BUYING TIP   Use any combination of seasonal fruit for this recipe.

□

OPPOSITE

FRESH FRUIT
PASTRIES

SERVES 4

FRUIT MILLEFEUILLES

*Served with a fresh raspberry sauce garnished with
diced kiwi fruit, these light pastries make a dessert that
never fails to please.*

Step 5

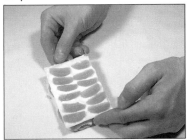

Step 5

☐ 12 oz puff paste, homemade or shop bought
☐ ½ cup heavy cream   ☐ 5 tbsps pastry cream
☐ 1 tsp any orange liqueur   ☐ 2 kiwis   ☐ 5 clementines

1. Roll out the dough very thinly to fit two dampened cookie sheets and prick the dough all over with a fork. Bake in a hot oven (400°F) for about 10-15 minutes.

2. Whip the cream and fold it into the pastry cream, along with the orange liqueur.

3. Peel the kiwis and slice into rounds. Peel and section the clementines, removing the skin from each segment.

4. Cut each cooled puff paste sheet into six equal portions.

5. Divide the cream evenly between the twelve portions, spreading it smoothly. Decorate four of these portions with the clementine segments, and another four with the kiwi slices, reserving a little of each fruit for decorating the finished pastries.

6. Top each clementine portion first with a kiwi portion and then with a plain portion. Decorate each pastry with the reserved fruit and serve.

☐ TIME   Preparation takes 20 minutes and cooking takes approximately 15 minutes.

☐ SERVING IDEA   Serve with a fresh raspberry sauce and diced kiwi fruit.

☐ COOK'S TIP   For a slightly sweeter cream filling whip in a little sugar.

☐

OPPOSITE

FRUIT
MILLEFEUILLES

PETS DE NONE

This intriguingly named recipe is for a version of French fritters – small, rich doughnuts that taste as delicious with coffee as for dessert.

Step 5

Step 5

Step 6

☐ ½ cup water ☐ 2 tbsps butter ☐ 1 pinch salt ☐ 1 tsp sugar
☐ 4 tbsps all-purpose flour ☐ 2 eggs ☐ Oil for deep-frying
☐ Confectioners' sugar and cinnamon

1. Make the dough in the same way as for choux paste: bring the water to a boil with the butter, salt and sugar.

2. When the water is boiling, add all the flour at once and beat the mixture vigorously. Continue to beat the batter continuously for 1 minute over a low heat.

3. Remove the mixture from the heat and beat in the first egg. When this is completely incorporated, beat in the second egg to obtain a smooth, elastic dough.

4. Heat the oil for deep-frying. Place the dough in a pastry bag with a plain metal tip.

5. When the oil is hot, squeeze out small dough balls from the pastry bag onto a spatula then use a second spatula or a knife to slide the balls off into the hot oil. Turn the pets de none during cooking, so that they cook evenly all over.

6. Using a slotted spoon, remove the cooked pets de none, drain them for 1 minute on paper towels and serve them immediately, sprinkled with sifted confectioners' sugar and cinnamon.

☐ TIME   Preparation takes 35 minutes and cooking takes approximately 10 minutes.

☐ VARIATION   Roll the pets de none in granulated sugar instead of confectioners' sugar and cinnamon.

☐ WATCHPOINT   When the eggs are added to the choux paste mixture, this will become sticky and separate. Beat the mixture well, to restore smoothness.

☐ SERVING IDEA   Serve with a custard sauce flavored with either cinnamon or vanilla.

☐

OPPOSITE

PETS DE NONE

GALETTE DES ROIS

*This pastry, which translates as "kings' cake," is traditionally
served in France at Epiphany, when a charm is baked into it
and the finder is entitled to be king, or queen, of the festivities.*

Step 4

Step 5

Step 6

Step 7

□ 4 tbsps softened butter   □ 4 tbsps sugar   □ 1 egg
□ 8 tbsps ground almonds   □ 2 tbsps pastry cream
□ 1 tsp rum   □ 1 lb puff paste   □ 1 egg, beaten

1. Cream together the butter and sugar, adding the egg and
ground almonds to obtain a thick almond cream.

2. Mix in the pastry cream and the rum until thoroughly
combined.

3. Roll out the dough thinly and cut into eight circles of which four
should be slightly larger than the rest.

4. Place the four smaller circles on a greased cookie sheet. Prick
them all over with a fork. Place the cream in a pastry bag and pipe
over the center of the circles, leaving a wide edge all the way
round.

5. Brush a little beaten egg around the edges of the pastry circles.

6. Cover them with the larger circles, pressing the edges together
well then crimping them to seal the galettes completely.

7. Brush the tops with the remaining beaten egg to give the
cooked galettes a glossy finish. Cook in a very hot oven (440°F) for
approximately 20 minutes, until the galettes are golden brown.

□ TIME   Preparation takes about 30 minutes and cooking takes
approximately 25 minutes.

□

OPPOSITE

GALETTE DES

ROIS

—— SERVES 4 ——

PRALINE MILLEFEUILLE

*Alone, this pastry makes a sophisticated accompaniment to
tea or coffee; served with a custard sauce flavored with
praliné and chocolate chips, it makes a dessert fit for a king.*

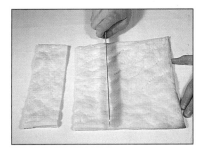

Step 5

Step 6

Step 7

□ 1 cup milk   □ 1 tbsp praliné powder   □ 2 egg yolks
□ 2½ tbsps sugar   □ 1½ tbsps flour, sifted   □ 2 cups puff paste
□ Confectioners' sugar   □ Cocoa powder

1. Boil up the milk with the praliné powder.

2. Beat together the egg yolks and the sugar until the mixture is light and lemon colored. Beat in the flour, mixing well.

3. Pour the hot milk over the above mixture, combine well and pour back into the saucepan. Bring to a boil, then lower the heat and cook, stirring continuously, until the mixture thickens. Set aside to cool.

4. Roll the dough out very thinly and place on a cookie sheet. Cook in a hot oven (400°F) for 10 minutes. Remove from the oven and allow to cool.

5. When the cooked dough has cooled, cut it first into strips and then into even-sized rectangles.

6. Spread a little of the pastry cream onto one of the rectangles.

7. Cover the first rectangle with another puff paste rectangle, spread over another layer of filling and finish with a third rectangle.

8. Continue until all the rectangles have been used up. Sift a little confectioners' sugar and cocoa over the top of the pastries to decorate.

□ TIME   Preparation takes about 35 minutes and cooking approximately 10 minutes.

□ VARIATION   2 cups of puff paste should yield 24 rectangles, sufficient for 8 small millefeuilles or one large one.

□ COOK'S TIP   Dampen the baking tray with a spray of water before placing the dough on it, to prevent this from sticking.

□

OPPOSITE

PRALINE
MILLEFEUILLE

─── SERVES 4 ───

MANGO BRICKS

*Phyllo dough encloses a tangy, fruit-flavored filling to make a
dessert that tastes perfect after a rich meal.*

Step 5

Step 6

Step 7

Step 8

□

OPPOSITE

MANGO BRICKS

□ 1 cup milk □ 2 egg yolks □ 2½ tbsps sugar
□ 1½ tbsps flour, sifted □ 1 tbsp coconut liqueur
□ 1 ripe mango □ 4 sheets phyllo dough
□ 3 kiwis □ 2 tbsps sugar
□ ¼ cup water □ 1 tbsp butter
□ 4 tbsps raspberry sauce/purée

---

1. Bring the milk to a boil. Beat together the egg yolks and sugar until the mixture is light and lemon colored. Add the flour and mix in well.

2. Pour the boiling milk over the above mixture, then return it to the saucepan, stirring continuously, and cook until thickened. Set aside to cool.

3. When the pastry cream is cool, mix in the coconut liqueur. Set aside.

4. Peel the mango and cut it into slices or small pieces.

5. Spread 1 tbsp of the pastry cream onto each sheet of dough to cover.

6. Place the mango in the centre of the dough sheets.

7. Fold in each side of the dough up and over the mango. Fold in the top and bottom.

8. Set the four even-sized 'bricks' aside until ready for cooking.

9. Peel the kiwi and remove the white core. Place the flesh in a food processor with the sugar and water and mix to a smooth purée. Chill in the refrigerator until needed.

10. Heat the butter in a pan until golden brown, add the bricks and sauté them until golden on both sides (approximately 2½ minutes on each side).

11. Place the cooked bricks on serving plates and decorate with the fruit purées.

□ TIME   Preparation takes about 20 minutes and cooking approximately 15 minutes.

□ COOK'S TIP   When cooking the mango bricks, use a long spatula and handle them carefully.

□ WATCHPOINT   The creamy filling sweats a little when spread on the phyllo dough; this helps to keep the dough damp.

—— SERVES 4 ——

APPLE STRUDEL

Homemade strudel dough is well worth the effort, but this dessert could be made equally successfully using shop-bought strudel or phyllo dough.

Step 2

Step 2

Step 2

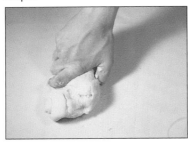

Step 3

☐

OPPOSITE

APPLE STRUDEL

STRUDEL DOUGH
- ☐ 1¼ cups all-purpose flour, sifted   ☐ Pinch salt
- ☐ ½ tsp oil   ☐ ½ tsp vinegar   ☐ ½ egg yolk
- ☐ 4 tbsps water (approximately)

FILLING
- ☐ 2 large apples   ☐ 2 tbsps butter   ☐ 1 tbsp currants
- ☐ 1 tbsp breadcrumbs   ☐ 1 tbsp ground almonds
- ☐ Cinnamon (to taste)

1. Begin making the strudel dough by mixing the salt into the well-sifted flour.

2. Add the oil, vinegar and egg yolk. Gradually add the water and work the ingredients together to form a ball of dough.

3. Knead well for 10 minutes.

4. Roll the dough in a damp dishtowel and allow to rest for 1 hour.

5. Peel and core the apples, then cut them into large cubes.

6. Heat the butter and sauté the apples, currants and breadcrumbs for 1 minute. Set aside to cool.

7. Mix the almonds into the apple mixture, sprinkle over cinnamon to taste and set aside.

8. When the dough has rested, roll it out as thinly as possible with a little flour.

9. Shape the dough into a large rectangle. Spread the apple filling down the center and roll up jelly-roll fashion.

10. Bake in a hot oven (400°F) for about 10 minutes. Cut into slices, using a serrated knife, and serve warm.

☐ TIME   Preparation takes about 45 minutes, cooking takes about 35 minutes and the strudel dough should rest for 1 hour before being rolled out.

☐ WATCHPOINT   The strudel dough is traditionally stretched out by hand. However, this is a very delicate method and very good results can be obtained by rolling it out, pressing down quite hard on the rolling pin.

☐ SERVING IDEA   Serve with a caramel-flavored custard sauce.

---- SERVES 4 ----

COCONUT BABA

A baba is traditionally flavored with rum and served with tea, but this variation is just as delicious served as a dessert.

Step 2

Step 2

Step 3

Step 4

☐ 2 cups all-purpose flour   ☐ 1 tsp yeast
☐ 5 tbsps warm water   ☐ 2 eggs   ☐ 4 tsps sugar
☐ Scant teaspoon salt   ☐ 1 cup water   ☐ ⅔ cup sugar
☐ ¼ cup melted butter
☐ 2 tbsps melted butter, for greasing   ☐ 2 tbsps coconut liqueur
☐ Melted chocolate, thinned with a little milk
☐ Thin slices of fresh coconut

1. Place the flour in a bowl, add the yeast with the 5 tbsps warm water.

2. Add the eggs, the 4 tsps sugar and the salt. Mix all the ingredients into a dough and then knead for 5 minutes.

3. Once the mixture is kneaded, add the remaining water, sugar and the ¼ cup melted butter, mixing them in well to obtain an elastic dough.

4. Use the 2 tbsps melted butter to grease one large or four small mold(s) and then fill two-thirds full with the dough.

5. Leave the dough to rise in a warm place for 45-60 minutes, until it reaches the top of the mold(s).

6. Bake the baba(s) in a hot oven (400°F) for 20-25 minutes. Remove the baba(s) from the oven, turn out and allow to cool a little.

7. Brush the coconut liqueur over the baba(s) while these are still warm. Allow to cool completely.

8. Serve the baba(s) with a little of the thinned melted chocolate and the coconut slices.

☐ TIME   Preparation takes about 35 minutes, plus 45-60 minutes rising time, and cooking takes approximately 20 minutes.

☐ WATCHPOINT   The dough has been sufficiently well kneaded when it leaves the sides of the bowl clean.

☐

OPPOSITE

COCONUT BABA

——— SERVES 4 ———

PRALINE SPONGE CAKE

This extravagant dessert cake is well worth its slightly time-consuming assembly and will earn you many compliments.

Step 2

Step 2

Step 3

□

OPPOSITE

PRALINE
SPONGE CAKE

SPONGE CAKE
□ 4 eggs □ ⅔ cup sugar □ 1¼ cups sifted all-purpose flour
□ 2 tbsps butter, melted □ Butter, for greasing □ Extra flour

PRALINÉ CREAM FILLING
□ 1 package gelatine □ 5½ tbsps sugar □ 3 egg yolks
□ 4 tsps flour □ 2 cups milk □ 5½ tbsps praliné
□ ¾ cup heavy cream □ 2 tbsps crushed praliné
□ Whipped cream and crushed praliné, to decorate

1. Grease a cake pan and dust the inside with a little flour, shaking out out any excess.

2. In a bowl, beat the eggs with the sugar. Place the bowl over a pan of simmering water and beat the mixture until it increases in volume and thickens. Remove the bowl from the heat and continue to beat the eggs until they have cooled and the mixture forms threads when dropped from a spoon.

3. Gently mix in first the flour and then the melted butter.

4. Fill the prepared cake pan three quarters full and bake the sponge in a moderate oven (325°F) for approximately 25 minutes, testing for doneness in the usual way. Turn out onto a wire rack and allow to cool. When completely cool, slice the sponge horizontally into four equal layers.

5. Meanwhile, to make the cream filling, soften the gelatin in a little cold water.

6. Mix together the sugar, egg yolks and flour. Bring the milk to a boil with the praliné, stirring to dissolve the latter, then pour it over the above egg yolk mixture and mix together well. Return the mixture to the saucepan and stir over a low heat until thickened. Set aside.

7. Stir the gelatin into the cream filling, then allow this to cool for 15 minutes, stirring occasionally.

8. Whip the cream until stiff, then fold it gently but thoroughly into the filling together with the crushed praliné.

9. Place one sponge layer on a serving plate, spread a quarter of the cream filling over it, then top with another sponge layer. Continue in this way, finishing with the final quarter of cream filling. Using a spatula to give a smooth finish, spread the cream over the top and sides of the cake.

10. Chill the cake in the refrigerator for 2 hours. Before serving, decorate with a little whipped cream and crushed praliné.

□ TIME Preparation takes about 1 hour 30 minutes and cooking takes approximately 25 minutes.

APPLE CAKE

This apple cake is a Germanic-inspired dessert that tastes equally delicious whether served with custard as a dessert or alone with coffee.

Step 2

Step 3

Step 4

☐ 2 large apples   ☐ 1 cup all-purpose flour   ☐ ½ cup sugar
☐ 2 tsps baking powder   ☐ 2 eggs   ☐ 1 pinch salt
☐ ½ cup melted butter   ☐ 2 tsps butter

1. Peel, core and dice the apples.

2. Beat together the flour, sugar, baking powder, eggs and salt.

3. Beat in the ½ cup melted butter.

4. Stir in the diced apple.

5. Butter a cake pan with the 2 tsps butter, pour in the cake batter and bake in a moderate oven (350°F) for about 35 minutes.

☐ TIME   Preparation takes about 15 minutes and cooking takes approximately 35 minutes.

☐ COOK'S TIP   Sprinkle the cake with cinnamon just before baking.

☐ SERVING IDEA   Accompany the cake with a cinnamon-flavored custard sauce and cider to drink.

☐ WATCHPOINT   Even if you use a non-stick cake pan, buttering it makes the cake easier to turn out.

☐

OPPOSITE

APPLE CAKE

--- SERVES 4 ---

CRÊPE CAKE

This layered dessert is a real dinner-party spectacular – and extremely rich and filling!

Step 4

Step 4

Step 5

Step 5

☐ 2 cups all-purpose flour ☐ 1 pinch salt ☐ 3 eggs
☐ 1 tbsp plum liqueur ☐ 4 tbsps sugar ☐ 2 cups milk
☐ 4 tbsps butter, softened ☐ 5 tbsps whipped cream
☐ 5 tbsps chestnut purée
☐ 1 tbsp maraschino, or other sweet liqueur ☐ Oil

1. To make the crêpe batter, mix together the flour, salt, eggs, plum liqueur and sugar. Add the milk gradually, beating continuously to ensure there are no lumps.

2. When all the ingredients are mixed well, beat in the softened butter. Set aside to rest for at least 15 minutes.

3. While the mixture is resting, fold the cream into the chestnut purée, stir in the maraschino and leave to chill in the refrigerator.

4. Cook the crêpes in a lightly greased frying pan, regreasing the pan between each crêpe. Allow the cooked crêpes to cool.

5. Spread a layer of chestnut filling on one of the crêpes, then top with another crêpe. Continue layering the crêpes and filling in this way until all the crêpes have been used.

6. Chill well in the refrigerator before serving. To serve, slice into portions like a traditional cake.

☐ TIME   Preparation takes 20 minutes and cooking takes approximately 35 minutes, plus extra chilling time.

☐ SERVING IDEA   Serve with custard sauce flavored with maraschino and chopped candied chestnuts.

☐ COOK'S TIP   The filling between each pancake should be very thin and smooth.

☐

OPPOSITE

CRÊPE CAKE

KUGELHOPF

This Continental yeasted cake is ideal for serving at teatime.

Step 3

Step 4

Step 5

Step 7

- ☐ 4½ cups all-purpose flour ☐ 1 cup warm milk
- ☐ 4 tsps yeast ☐ 2 tbsps plum liqueur ☐ ½ cup raisins
- ☐ ¼ tsp salt ☐ 2 eggs ☐ Scant ½ cup sugar
- ☐ ¾ cup butter, softened
- ☐ 5 tbsps slivered almonds ☐ Butter for greasing

1. Mix together ⅔ cup flour with half the warm milk and all the yeast and leave for 1 hour in a warm place.

2. Pour the liqueur over the raisins and leave to marinate.

3. Mix the salt, eggs, sugar and remaining milk into the remaining flour.

4. Knead the dough for at least five minutes.

5. Knead the softened butter and the yeast mixture into the dough until well mixed.

6. Set the dough aside in a warm place for one hour, or until it has risen and tripled in volume.

7. When the dough has tripled in size, mix in the raisins and almonds.

8. Grease a kugelhopf, or brioche, mold with melted butter. Place the dough evenly in the mold.

9. Bake in a moderate oven (350°F) for 45 minutes. Allow to rest in the pan for 15 minutes before turning out.

☐ TIME Preparation takes about 40 minutes, plus 2 hours resting/rising time, and cooking takes approximately 45 minutes.

☐ VARIATION The almonds could be replaced with walnuts, and the weight of the raisins increased slightly to compensate.

☐ WATCHPOINT The more you knead the dough the lighter and fluffier your kugelhopf will be.

☐

OPPOSITE

KUGELHOPF

POUND CAKE

*A plain cake that complements fruit salads to perfection, and
is also a welcome addition to the afternoon tea table.*

Step 2

Step 3

☐ 1¼ cups softened butter ☐ 1½ cups sugar ☐ ½ tsps vanilla
extract ☐ 5 eggs ☐ 1 tbsp orange flower water
☐ 2 tsps baking powder ☐ 3 cups all-purpose flour

1. Cream together the butter, sugar and vanilla.

2. Beat in the eggs one at a time, together with the orange flower
water and the baking powder. Gradually beat in the flour to obtain
a thick batter.

3. Pour the cake batter into either a non-stick or a greased and
lined loaf pan and bake in a moderate oven (350°F) for about 45
minutes, testing for doneness in the usual way.

4. Turn out onto a cake rack to cool.

☐ TIME   Preparation takes 15 minutes and cooking takes
approximately 45 minutes.

☐ VARIATION   Chopped hazelnuts or walnuts may be added to
the cake batter.

☐

OPPOSITE

POUND CAKE

——— SERVES 4 ———

SPONGE CAKES WITH BLUEBERRIES

A steamed sponge cake forms the basis of this deliciously different dessert.

□ 1¼ cups all-purpose flour, sifted   □ 3 tbsps sugar
□ 1 tbsp baking powder   □ 2 eggs   □ 1½ tbsps oil
□ Scant ½ cup milk   □ 1 tbsp rice alcohol
□ 4 tbsps blueberry jam

Step 1

Step 2

Step 3

Step 3

1. Mix together the flour and sugar.

2. Mix in the baking powder and the eggs.

3. Add 1 tbsp of the oil and then add the milk gradually, mixing well after each addition to obtain a smooth paste.

4. Grease four ramekins with the remaining oil and divide the mixture evenly between them.

5. Place in a steamer, cover and cook for 20 minutes.

6. Add the rice alcohol to the jam and stir well to obtain a sauce.

7. Turn the sponges out of the ramekins as soon as they are cooked, slice them and serve with the jam sauce.

□ TIME   Preparation takes about 20 minutes and cooking also takes about 20 minutes.

□ VARIATION   This cake batter can be used in other recipes to replace more traditional mixtures. Different flavored jams could be used in this recipe.

□ COOK'S TIP   If a slightly buttery flavor is preferred, grease the ramekins with butter rather than oil.

□

OPPOSITE

SPONGE CAKES
WITH
BLUEBERRIES

SERVES 8

FRUIT CAKE

A good standby in any store cupboard, a well-flavored fruit cake can be served with a fruit salad or ice cream or brought out to serve with coffee at the end of a light meal.

Step 2

Step 2

Step 3

Step 5

- □ 1½ cups candied fruit □ 1 cup raisins □ 2 tbsps rum
- □ ⅞ cup softened butter □ ⅞ cup sugar □ 3 eggs
- □ 2½ cups all-purpose flour □ 1 tsp baking powder
- □ 2 tsps butter, for greasing

1. Marinate the candied fruit and the raisins in the rum for 2 hours.

2. Cream together the sugar and butter until light. Beat in the eggs, baking powder and flour.

3. Add the marinated fruit and raisins, together with the marinade, to the cake batter and mix in well.

4. Grease a cake pan.

5. Turn the cake batter into the greased pan. Tap the pan to eliminate any bubbles in the batter, level the top and bake in a hot oven (400°F) for about 45 minutes, testing for doneness in the usual way.

6. When cooked, allow the cake to cool slightly in the pan, before turning it out onto a wire rack to cool completely.

□ TIME   Preparation takes about 20 minutes, plus 2 hours marinating time, and cooking takes approximately 45 minutes.

□ COOK'S TIP   Use a serrated knife to slice the cake, as it has a crumbly texture.

□ VARIATION   The rum may be replaced with another liqueur. The cake can also be made using a combination of finely diced dried fruit: figs, dates, pears, apricots, etc.

□

OPPOSITE

FRUIT CAKE

— SERVES 6 —

CAT'S TONGUES

*These cookies are a classic accompaniment to ice cream
or fruit desserts, and are also traditionally served with
afternoon tea.*

Step 3

Step 3

Step 5

- ⅔ cup softened butter   □ 2 cups confectioners' sugar
- □ 1 tsp vanilla extract   □ 5 egg whites
- □ 2 cups all-purpose flour, sifted

---

1. Cream the butter with the confectioners' sugar and the vanilla extract.

2. Add the egg whites one by one, alternating with the flour until a firm dough is obtained.

3. Place the dough in a pastry bag with a plain metal tip. Pipe even-sized strips of dough onto a greased cookie sheet. Leave space between the cookies as they spread during baking.

4. Bake in a very hot oven (410°F) for 10-15 minutes: the edges should be golden brown but the centers still light.

5. When cooked, removed the cookies from the oven, allow them to cool slightly on the cookie sheet, then use a spatula to lift them onto a wire rack and allow to cool completely.

□ TIME   Preparation takes about 15 minutes and cooking takes 10-15 minutes.

□ WATCHPOINT   Cooking time varies according to the size and thickness of the cookies; they are cooked when the edges are golden brown.

□

OPPOSITE

CAT'S TONGUES

CHOCOLATE TRUFFLES

*These rich chocolate truffles should be served with coffee at
the end of a special meal.*

Step 3

Step 4

Step 4

☐ 1½ cups bitter chocolate ☐ 4 tbsps butter ☐ 2 tbsps sugar
☐ 1 tsp rum ☐ 3 tbsps crème fraîche
☐ Cocoa powder, sifted onto a plate

---

1. Melt the chocolate with the butter, sugar and rum in a bowl
either over a pan of simmering water or in the microwave.

2. Beat the above ingredients together well and stir in the crème
fraîche. Place the truffle mixture in the refrigerator for 2 hours to
harden.

3. Using a melon baller or a spoon, scoop out small balls of truffle
mixture, or form into other shapes.

4. Toss the truffles in the sifted cocoa powder as they are scooped
out. Store in a cool place until needed.

☐ TIME   Preparation takes about 20 minutes, plus at least 2 hours
chilling time.

☐ VARIATION   Marinate raisins in rum and add to the truffle
mixture at Step 2.

☐

OPPOSITE

CHOCOLATE

TRUFFLES

— SERVES 4 —

PALM LEAF COOKIES

Palm leaf cookies originated in France, where they can still be bought in pâtisseries all over the country. They make a perfect accompaniment to ice creams and sherbets or to fruit desserts.

Step 2

Step 3

Step 4

Step 5

☐ 8 oz puff paste, homemade or shop bought ☐ 3 tbsps sugar
☐ Confectioners' sugar

1. Roll the puff paste out to form a rectangle.

2. Sprinkle a work surface with half the sugar.

3. Place the dough on the sugared surface, and sprinkle over the remaining sugar. Roll lightly over the dough so that the sugar sticks to it.

4. Roll each of the two ends of the dough up toward the middle, and place the rolled dough in the freezer for 20 minutes, to make it easier to slice.

5. Remove from the freezer and slice the rolled dough to the desired thickness to form the palm cookies.

6 Place the cookies on a dampened cookie sheet. Bake in a hot oven (400°F) for 20 minutes, or until golden brown.

7. Allow the cookies to cool, then sprinkle with confectioners' sugar before serving.

☐ TIME   Preparation takes about 15 minutes, plus 20 minutes resting time, and cooking takes approximately 20 minutes.

☐

OPPOSITE

PALM LEAF
COOKIES

—— MAKES 30 COOKIES ——

COCONUT TILE COOKIES

These homemade cookies provide the perfect finishing touch to a wide variety of desserts and are particularly good as an accompaniment to ice creams or sherbets.

Step 3

Step 4

Step 4

☐ ½ cup sugar   ☐ 2 egg whites   ☐ ½ cup all-purpose flour
☐ ¼ cup melted butter   ☐ ½ cup ground coconut
☐ Extra butter for greasing

1. Beat the sugar into the egg whites.

2. Add the flour and butter, beating well. Beat in the coconut, then allow to rest for 10 minutes.

3. Butter cookie sheets. Use the back of a spoon to spread out 1 tbsp of batter for each cookie.

4. Cook each tray of cookies for 3-4 minutes in a preheated hot oven (400°F). Remove the cookies from the trays with a spatula and immediately shape them around a rolling pin. They will cool and harden very quickly. Slide onto a wire rack to cool.

5. Repeat the cooking and cooling operation until all the cookie batter has been used up.

☐ TIME   Preparation takes about 10 minutes and the complete cooking time takes approximately 35 minutes.

☐ WATCHPOINT   Cooking time depends on the thickness of the cookies. As soon as they color lightly around the edges, they are done.

☐ VARIATION   The ground coconut can be replaced with ground almonds.

☐

OPPOSITE

COCONUT TILE
COOKIES

—— SERVES 6 ——

MACAROONS

*Perfect served with afternoon tea or with coffee at the end of
a meal, these delicious little cookies also make a good
accompaniment to desserts of all kinds.*

Step 2

Step 2

Step 3

Step 4

☐ 2 egg whites   ☐ Salt   ☐ ⅞ cup sugar
☐ 1 cup ground almonds

1. Beat the egg whites with a pinch of salt until foamy, then gradually add the sugar, beating continuously until the whites are stiff.

2. Fold the ground almonds into the egg whites to obtain a thick paste; the egg whites will lose some of their volume in the process.

3. Place the paste in a pastry bag with a plain metal tip. Pipe small balls of paste onto cookie sheets lined with buttered waxed paper, spacing them quite far apart. Do this in batches, if necessary.

4. Cook in a moderate oven (340°F) until lightly colored, remove from the oven and use a spatula to transfer them to a cake rack to cool. Once cool, they become hard and crunchy.

☐ TIME   Preparation takes about 15 minutes and cooking takes approximately 10 minutes per batch.

☐ WATCHPOINT   Space the cookies quite far apart on the sheets, as they spread during cooking.

☐

OPPOSITE

MACAROONS

— SERVES 4 —

FLORENTINE COOKIES

Originally from Italy, as their name suggests, Florentines are a good accompaniment to a plain dessert, such as ice cream, but are just as tasty served with a cup of coffee at the very end of a meal.

□ ¾ cup sugar   □ 2 tbsps honey   □ ½ cup water
□ ¼ cup heavy cream   □ ½ cup candied fruit
□ 2 tbsps currants   □ ¼ cup sliced or slivered almonds
□ 4 oz unsweetened chocolate   □ ¼ cup milk

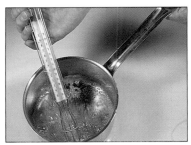

Step 1

Step 3

Step 5

1. Place the sugar, honey and water in a saucepan and bring to a boil. Using a candy thermometer, boil the syrup to 245°F then remove from the heat.

2. Pour in the cream and combine thoroughly.

3. Add the fruit, currants and almonds and stir together well.

4. Spoon a little of this cookie mixture into well greased cookie molds or form little patties of the mixture on a well greased cookie sheet. Cook each batch in a hot oven (400°F) for approximately 10 minutes, or until the cookies are golden brown.

5. Remove the cookies from the oven and use a spatula to scrape the cooked edges back towards the centers. Allow to cool for 2 to 3 minutes before removing them from the molds or sheets. Either cool on a rack or round a wooden rolling pin to give a rounded shape.

6. In a bowl, melt the chocolate and milk together either over a pan of boiling water or in a microwave oven. Dip the Florentines in the chocolate mixture to coat half of each cookie. Allow to harden and then serve.

□ TIME   Preparation takes about 20 minutes, cooking takes approximately 20 minutes and resting time is about 20 minutes.

□ WATCHPOINT   The cookies bubble during cooking, but this stops once they have cooled down. Watch the cookies carefully during cooking – it is impossible to turn them out if they overcook. Allowing the cookies to cool before removing them from the molds is important; if they are too hot, they will fall apart.

□

OPPOSITE

FLORENTINE
COOKIES